Playing to Win at Bridge contains a selection of entertaining and instructive problems from actual play. For each problem two hands are shown together with the bidding and the play to the first few tricks. The reader is then invited to take over and plan the play or defense before turning to the solution where all four hands are given.

As one would expect from a master teacher, the emphasis is on practical problems of the sort that are frequently encountered in a game. In the handling of these common situation lies the secret of playing to win.

Ron Klinger is not only an international player, a winner of many prestigious bridge championships and a well-known leading bridge journalist. He is also a Master of Laws, with First Class Honors, and has years of experience in teaching bridge at all levels. He brings to his books the sharpness of a trained legal mind, together with the authority of a Grand Master and the understanding of a top teacher.

"*Playing to Win at Bridge* is as good a quiz book as has ever appeared. The feature that distinguishes this collection from most others is the absence of special themes. Instead of examples of well known ideas, the author presents truly practical situations. As declarer, you are more likely to be wondering how best to combine the different chances than how to operate an esoteric squeeze. On defense, you must worry about your aces getting away before you turn your thoughts to complex coups. In short, the questions emphasize those aspects of bridge play that are truly important at the table. Our quibbles with the analysis are minor, and we recommend the book as outstanding of its kind."

— *The Bridge World*

Other books by Ron Klinger
published by Houghton Mifflin Company

Guide To Better Bridge
Guide To Better Card Play
100 Winning Bridge Tips
Five-Card Majors
Standard Bridge Flipper

by Hugh Kelsey and Ron Klinger

Instant Guide To Bridge

Standard American Edition

PLAYING
TO WIN AT
BRIDGE

*Practical Problems for
the Improving Player*

RON KLINGER

*A Master Bridge Series title
in conjunction with Peter Crawley*

Houghton Mifflin Company
Boston   New York
1993

Libraray of Congress Cataloguing-in-Publication Data
Klinger, Ron.
Playing to win at bridge : practical problems for the improving player /
Ron Klinger. — Standard American ed.
p.   cm.
"A Master bridge series title in conjunction with Peter Crawley."
Originally published: London : Ward Lock, 1976.
ISBN: 0-395-65666-4
1. Contract bridge.   I. Title. II. Series: Master bridge series.
GV1282.3.K63 1993
795.415 — dc20   92-35309
                      CIP

Printed in the United States of America

BP 10 9 8 7 6 5 4 3 2 1

To Suzie

Contents

Preface

It is one of the harder facts of life to accept that skill in bridge is based to a great extent on experience. No amount of theoretical study and technical knowledge can make up for a failure to recognize the problem presented by a new deal. The advantage of the player who 'has been there before' is considerable; the experienced player has an immense storehouse of familiar situations to draw upon.

This collection of bridge problems is an attempt to equip the not-so-experienced player with the everyday situations of rubber and tournament bridge, so that he may add to his present storehouse. Having met a situation in these pages and having grasped the reasoning behind the solution, a player will be better able to deal with similar problems when they actually arise.

This is not a book of esoteric problems or complex squeeze positions. You will be hard pressed to find in it standard textbook hands or 'sure trick' plays, which, though important, occur only rarely at the table. Rather, you may expect to find the countless irritating problems which crop up every day, and the clues by which they may be solved. This is a book of practical problems taken from real life. You may take comfort from the fact that on almost every hand somebody went wrong, failing to make the contract or failing to find the best defence.

You will not find any common thread running through a group of hands in this book. You will not see, for example, one section devoted to endplays, another to trump control plays and a third to card-reading problems. That is not what happens at the bridge table, where there is no rhyme or reason to the order in which problems occur. The hands are intended to simulate normal playing conditions, although you have the advantage of knowing that you face a problem on each deal. At the table, one of the hardest things is to recognize that a problem exists. The world is full of expert dummy players and brilliant defenders five seconds after the play of the hand has finished. It is the ability to solve the problem five seconds *before* the critical moment that is the hallmark of the top player.

The hands are grouped into three categories according to difficulty— elementary, intermediate and advanced. Except where otherwise stated, bidding should be taken to be along standard Acol lines. Assume that normal defensive methods are used, with standard leads (king from ace-king) and standard signals.

The bidding is almost invariably presented as it happened at the table. The opponents' bidding is often less than perfect and at times frankly shocking, but isn't that what happens in real life? Thank heavens we do not sit down to play against the Blue Team all the time. Similarly, the contracts reached by you and your partner are not always ideal and your bidding sequences are not always what they should be, but then you and your present partner are not the world's best bidders, are you? (If you *are* the world's best bidders, please assume you have been asked to play the hand for someone else.)

Particulars of dealer, vulnerability and setting are given for each problem along with the actual play up to the critical point. Where any additional information about the auction is required, it is provided. But that does not mean that all additional information is relevant. As happens at the table, you receive a lot of excess information and you have to sift out from the available data what is relevant and what is not. Is it the opponents' bidding? Is it partner's lead? Is it the way declarer is tackling the hand? Is it partner's signalling? Or is it just a matter of card combinations?

The elements of good declarer play and competent defence are analogous to the elements of good detective work. Sherlock Holmes would have made a splendid bridge player, for he had the ability to sort out from a morass of clues those few that pointed towards the correct solution. Facility in logical reasoning is a matter of training and practice. At some time in the future, after bringing in a difficult contract or a tough defence, you may find yourself saying: 'Elementary, my dear partner!'

A word is needed about the presentation of the problems. Where a card is shown in **bold face** it means that the trick was won with that card. When a discard is made or when someone ruffs, this is indicated in *italics*. For each trick the player who makes the lead is named, along with the next three cards in rotation. For example:

South leads ◇K: two, three, seven

This means that South led the king of diamonds and won the trick **(bold face)**, and that West played the two, North the three and East the seven of diamonds. Here is an actual problem, No. 42:

Pairs, dealer South,
East-West vulnerable.

♠: J 10 5 3
♡: 8 6 5 2
◇: 5
♣: A 10 4 3

SOUTH	WEST	NORTH	EAST
1 NT*	Pass	Pass	Pass

* 12–14 points

♠: Q 9 7 4
♡: K Q 9
◇: K J 8 7
♣: K 6

The play:
1 West leads ♣5: three, **king**, eight
2 East leads ◇7: **queen**, ten, five
3 **South leads** ♠A: eight, three, seven

10

4 South leads ♠K: *West discards ♣2*
5 South leads ♠6: *West discards ◇3,* ♠J *from dummy . . . .*

How should East defend?

At trick one West leads the five of clubs, the three is played from the table, East wins the king and South follows with the eight. East returns the seven of diamonds and the trick is won by South's queen, West playing the ten and dummy the five. South plays off the ace and king of spades and West discards the two of clubs on the second round. Then comes a spade to dummy's jack, West discarding the three of diamonds, and at this point East has to decide how to plan his defence.

After a little practice you should have no trouble in following the play on each hand.

It is a good idea to use paper and pencil when tackling each problem and to write down a definite answer. That will give a better indication of your accuracy than the inflated idea you may acquire by simply thinking about possible lines of play, then looking at the answer and saying to yourself: 'Oh, yes, of course that's what I would have done.' Your aim should be improved technique, not self-delusion.

I hope you will enjoy the problems. I know you will be a better player after studying them.

Part one Elementary level

A competent player should score at least 90% in this section and should not require more than two or three minutes to come up with the winning line for each problem.

1

Dealer North,
both sides vulnerable.

The bidding:

WEST	NORTH	EAST	SOUTH
	Pass	Pass	2 NT
Pass	3 NT	End	

♠: 8 3
♡: Q 10 3
◇: Q 7 6 2
♣: 9 8 3 2

♠: A K 6
♡: A K J 4
◇: J 4
♣: K Q J 5

The play:
1 West leads ♠Q: three, two . . . .

Plan South's play.

2

♠: J 7 6 2
♡: J 9
◇: K 5 4 3
♣: A 6 2

♠: A K 10 4
♡: K 6
◇: J 8 7
♣: 9 7 5 3

Pairs, dealer North,
neither side vulnerable.

The bidding:

SOUTH	WEST	NORTH	EAST
		Pass	Pass
1 ♡	1 ♠	1 NT	Pass
3 ♡	Pass	4 ♡	End

The play:
1 **West leads ♠K:** two, three, five
2 West plays ♣7: **ace,** eight, ten
3 ♡J is led from dummy: eight, two, **king.**

Plan West's defence.

3

Dealer South,
neither side vulnerable.

The bidding:

SOUTH	WEST	NORTH	EAST
1 NT	Pass	3 NT	End

♠: J 3
♡: 6 4
◇: Q J 10 6 3
♣: A J 6 4

♠: A 10 5
♡: Q J
◇: A 8 4 2
♣: K Q 3 2

The final contract is a little inelegant, but all is not lost since West leads the four of spades. How do you play to maximize your chances of success?

4

♠: K Q J 4
♡: Q 8 5
◇: Q 10 7 4 3
♣: 9

♠: 8 6 2
♡: 9
◇: 8 5
♣: A Q 8 7 6 4 3

Dealer North,
both sides vulnerable.

The bidding:

WEST	NORTH	EAST	SOUTH
	Pass	Pass	1 ♠
2 ♣	3 ♠	Pass	4 ♠
Pass	Pass	Pass	

The play:
1 West leads ♡9: five, **ace**, six
2 East returns ♡10: seven, *ruffed with ♠6*, eight.

How should West continue?

1. Maximizing chances

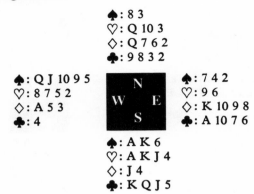

♠: 8 3
♡: Q 10 3
◇: Q 7 6 2
♣: 9 8 3 2

♠: Q J 10 9 5
♡: 8 7 5 2
◇: A 5 3
♣: 4

♠: 7 4 2
♡: 9 6
◇: K 10 9 8
♣: A 10 7 6

♠: A K 6
♡: A K J 4
◇: J 4
♣: K Q J 5

Trap 1: Don't duck the opening lead. It would be all right to do so if you could be sure of a spade continuation, but if the defence were to switch to diamonds you could lose one spade, three diamonds and a club.

Trap 2: After winning ♠A, don't play the king of clubs. That would cost a trick if East began with ♣A singleton.

The correct line is to win ♠A, play ♡4 to dummy's ten and lead a small club, playing the king if East plays low. Then:

a) if the king loses to the ace, play the queen of clubs when you regain the lead and claim if the clubs are 3–2. If East began with 10 x x x, play the ♡J, overtake with dummy's queen and lead ♣9 for a finesse;

b) if the king of clubs holds, do *not* play ♡J to the queen to lead another club from dummy; that would fail on the layout above. Instead lay down the queen of clubs. If East has four clubs and takes the ace, you later cross to ♡Q and run ♣9. If East lets ♣Q win, you will cross at once to ♡Q and lead another club.

2. The sins of the auction may be visited on the defence

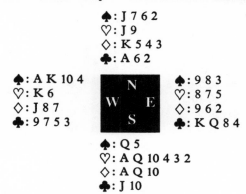

♠: J 7 6 2
♡: J 9
◇: K 5 4 3
♣: A 6 2

♠: A K 10 4
♡: K 6
◇: J 8 7
♣: 9 7 5 3

♠: 9 8 3
♡: 8 7 5
◇: 9 6 2
♣: K Q 8 4

♠: Q 5
♡: A Q 10 4 3 2
◇: A Q 10
♣: J 10

One of the most difficult areas of defence is that pertaining to the cashing of defensive tricks in the right order. It takes close co-operation and accurate count signals to make sure that the defenders cash all the tricks that are available. It will repay most partnerships to spend some time clarifying their agreements in this area.

Here it is important for West to cash the ace of spades before leading a second club. If West returns a club immediately South is likely to make four hearts. East will win and, placing West with five spades for his overcall, will almost certainly try to cash another club. South will ruff the third club and his spade loser will disappear on the thirteenth diamond.

West can be confident that the ace of spades will survive, for if East had begun with Q x x x in spades and a strong club holding (evident from his eight of clubs signal), he would have competed with two spades over one no trump.

3. Out of the rut

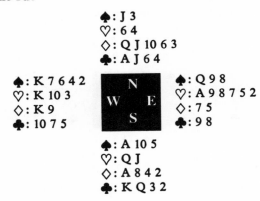

```
                    ♠ : J 3
                    ♡ : 6 4
                    ◇ : Q J 10 6 3
                    ♣ : A J 6 4

♠ : K 7 6 4 2                        ♠ : Q 9 8
♡ : K 10 3                           ♡ : A 9 8 7 5 2
◇ : K 9                              ◇ : 7 5
♣ : 10 7 5                           ♣ : 9 8

                    ♠ : A 10 5
                    ♡ : Q J
                    ◇ : A 8 4 2
                    ♣ : K Q 3 2
```

The routine play is a low spade from dummy in order to ensure two tricks
in the suit, but the desperate heart situation calls for other measures.
If the diamond finesse is working you'll have no problems, but what if
the finesse fails ? You want to encourage West to continue spades
rather than to find the heart switch.

Suppose you play the three of spades from dummy at trick one. Whether
East plays the queen or the eight, West will be able to work out that
you have a double stopper in spades. And when you cross to the ♣A
for the diamond finesse, West is likely to realize that you will make at
least nine tricks as soon as you regain the lead. He will therefore switch
to hearts, carefully unblocking the ten in the process.

But if you play the ♠J from dummy and win East's queen with the ace,
West will find it irresistible to infer that the ten is with East. On winning
the king of diamonds, West will underlead his king of spades in order to
avoid blocking the suit.

Keep an eye on West's face as you win with the ten. It will be a moment
to cherish.

4. Trust partner, but safety first

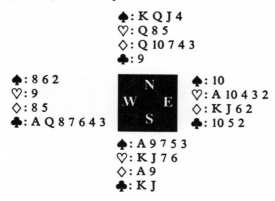

♠: K Q J 4
♡: Q 8 5
◇: Q 10 7 4 3
♣: 9

♠: 8 6 2
♡: 9
◇: 8 5
♣: A Q 8 7 6 4 3

♠: 10
♡: A 10 4 3 2
◇: K J 6 2
♣: 10 5 2

♠: A 9 7 5 3
♡: K J 7 6
◇: A 9
♣: K J

West should cash the ace of clubs before playing a diamond.

East's ♡10 return is a suit-preference request for a diamond return, but that does not mean that East must have the ace or that West should blindly follow instructions.

South is known to have started with K J x x in hearts (East's ace at trick one places the king with South, and his ten at trick two marks South with the jack). You can visualize what will happen on a diamond return if East does not have the ace. South will win, draw trumps in two rounds, and discard dummy's club on the fourth heart. He will thus make his contract if he can hold his diamond losers to one.

Cashing the club ace first is perfectly safe. The diamonds can wait, since South can have no way of disposing of any losers he may have in that suit.

Yes, five clubs is a good East–West contract, succeeding unless the opponents lead trumps initially, but that is no reason to let them make four spades.

5

Teams, dealer North,
both sides vulnerable.

♠: J 9 3
♡: A K Q J
◇: 9 6 2
♣: A K Q

The bidding:

WEST	NORTH	EAST	SOUTH
	1 ♡	Pass	1 NT
Pass	3 NT	End	

♠: A 7 4
♡: 6 5 3
◇: J 8 7
♣: J 8 3 2

West leads ♠6. Plan the play.

6

♠: K Q 7 2
♡: 8
◇: A Q J 7 3
♣: K 10 7

Teams, dealer East,
North-South vulnerable.

The bidding:

WEST	NORTH	EAST	SOUTH
		Pass	Pass
Pass	1 ◇	Pass	2 NT
Pass	3 NT	End	

♠: 8 6 4
♡: K 9 7 6 3
◇: K 9 6
♣: 9 5

The play:

1 West leads ♡6: eight, **ace,** four
2 East returns ♡J: South plays the queen . . . .

Plan West's defence.

7

Teams, dealer West,
North-South vulnerable.

The bidding:

WEST	NORTH	EAST	SOUTH
3 ♣	3 ◇	Pass	4 NT
Pass	5 ♡	Pass	6 NT
Pass	Pass	Pass	

♠: 7
♡: K J 4
◇: A 10 8 3 2
♣: A 7 4 2

♠: K Q J 10
♡: A Q 3
◇: K J 9 4
♣: K 6

The play:
1 West leads ♣Q: two, *East discards* ♡2, **king**
2 South leads ♠K: **East wins ♠A**
3 East returns ♠5: West follows.

Plan South's play.

8

♠: Q J 5
♡: K 8 4 2
◇: K J 7 6
♣: Q 6

♠: 8 3
♡: Q J 6 5
◇: A 8 3
♣: 10 9 8 4

Rubber, dealer South,
both sides vulnerable.

The bidding:

SOUTH	WEST	NORTH	EAST
1 ♠	Pass	2 NT	Pass
4 ♠	Pass	Pass	Pass

The play:
1 West leads ♣10: queen, **king,** five
2 East returns ♠4: six, eight, **queen**
3 ◇6 is led from dummy: five, queen, **ace.**

How should West proceed?

5. Don't be an automaton

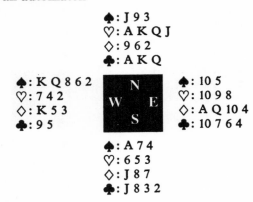

♠: J 9 3
♥: A K Q J
♦: 9 6 2
♣: A K Q

♠: K Q 8 6 2
♥: 7 4 2
♦: K 5 3
♣: 9 5

♠: 10 5
♥: 10 9 8
♦: A Q 10 4
♣: 10 7 6 4

♠: A 7 4
♥: 6 5 3
♦: J 8 7
♣: J 8 3 2

Normally the correct play with J 9 x in dummy opposite A x or A x x is to insert dummy's nine. This caters for the more frequent situations: West is more likely to have led from K 10 x x x or Q 10 x x x than from K Q x x x.

But circumstances alter cases. Here, if West has led from K 10 x x x or Q 10 x x x, you cannot, barring miracles, make the contract. East's honour will force out the ♠A, your only entry, before the clubs can be unblocked. After winning ♠A you can try returning a spade, of course, but only the rawest beginner in the West seat will play low. West can see that you will have nine tricks if ♠J wins, so he will naturally win the spade and switch to diamonds, putting you one down.

Your only legitimate chance is that West has underled the king and queen of spades, and you should therefore play the jack from dummy. If it wins, play off dummy's clubs, come to hand with the ♠A, and cash ♣J and the hearts for nine tricks.

If the ♠J is covered by East, you will have to play for the miracle. Duck in hand, win the spade return if it comes, cash dummy's club and heart winners and play a diamond, hoping for East's hand to be Q x, x x x x, A K Q, x x x x.

6. Out for a duck

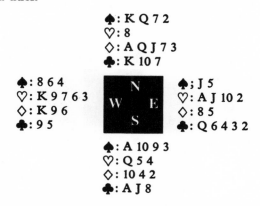

```
                    ♠: K Q 7 2
                    ♡: 8
                    ◇: A Q J 7 3
                    ♣: K 10 7
♠: 8 6 4                              ♠; J 5
♡: K 9 7 6 3                          ♡: A J 10 2
◇: K 9 6                              ◇: 8 5
♣: 9 5                               ♣: Q 6 4 3 2
                    ♠: A 10 9 3
                    ♡: Q 5 4
                    ◇: 10 4 2
                    ♣: A J 8
```

Sometimes it is correct to duck in defence in order to preserve communications with partner, but this isn't one of those times. If you duck, you can see the declarer making at least nine tricks and his contract. He will make one heart, five diamonds (since the finesse is working) and at least three tricks in the black suits even in the unlikely event that partner has an ace.

The tricks to defeat the contract must be taken now or not at all. You must win the king of hearts and continue the suit. If South began with Q 10 x or Q 10 x x in hearts there is nothing you can do about it.

After the hand you may compliment East on his proper return of the ♡J. The careless return of the ♡2 ('to give you the count, partner') would have blocked the suit.

It would of course be poor form to ask 'innocently' if North and South could have made six spades.

7. A sure thing

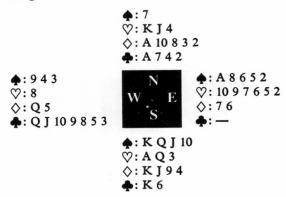

♠: 7
♡: K J 4
◇: A 10 8 3 2
♣: A 7 4 2

♠: 9 4 3
♡: 8
◇: Q 5
♣: Q J 10 9 8 5 3

♠: A 8 6 5 2
♡: 10 9 7 6 5 2
◇: 7 6
♣: —

♠: K Q J 10
♡: A Q 3
◇: K J 9 4
♣: K 6

A little knowledge is a dangerous thing. Crying: 'Aha, West has seven clubs and two spades, so he must be short in diamonds', the declarer played a diamond to the ace and finessed through East on the way back. One down!

Perhaps it would be more accurate to say that little knowledge is a dangerous thing. Although the odds favour East having length in diamonds, why accept any odds when the contract can be ensured simply by playing off your spades and hearts and finding out *exactly* how many diamonds West has?

On the actual hand, West shows out on the fourth spade and on the second heart, marking him with precisely two diamonds. If West proved to have only three cards in the major suits, you would know to play him for three diamonds as well, while if he showed up with five cards in the majors it would be clear that he could have no more than one diamond.

8. Needs must

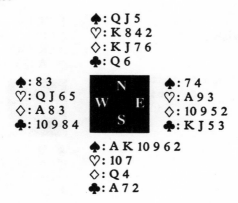

♠ : Q J 5
♡ : K 8 4 2
◇ : K J 7 6
♣ : Q 6

♠ : 8 3
♡ : Q J 6 5
◇ : A 8 3
♣ : 10 9 8 4

♠ : 7 4
♡ : A 9 3
◇ : 10 9 5 2
♣ : K J 5 3

♠ : A K 10 9 6 2
♡ : 10 7
◇ : Q 4
♣ : A 7 2

You must switch to the queen of hearts at trick four. If declarer has the ace of hearts, you will not beat four spades, for South will make six spade tricks (the jump to four spades must surely be based on a six-card suit), two hearts and two diamonds. His only losers will be two clubs and a diamond.

On anything but the heart return the declarer has an easy time, discarding a heart loser on the diamonds and ruffing his third club on the table. You don't know that East does have the ♡A, but you do know that you won't beat four spades unless he has it.

Perhaps you also noted South as a possible future partner. His careful duck at trick one was a precautionary measure which would have ensured the success of the contract if East had held the ace of diamonds. By ducking, declarer prevents West, the danger hand, from regaining the lead at a later stage to play a heart through the king. If declarer fails to duck, East, on winning the ace of diamonds, could put his partner in by underleading the jack of clubs.

9

Dealer South,
both sides vulnerable.

The bidding:

SOUTH	WEST	NORTH	EAST
2 ♡	Pass	3 ♣	Pass
4 ♡	Pass	6 ♡	End

♠: K J 4
♡: 10
◇: K 5 4
♣: A Q J 6 4 3

♠: Q 5 3
♡: A K Q J 8 7 6 2
◇: 9
♣: K

After the hand, a discussion with partner about the merits of **Blackwood** may be profitable.
Luckily, West leads the ten of clubs. Plan South's play.

10

Rubber, dealer South,
both sides vulnerable.

The bidding:

SOUTH	WEST	NORTH	EAST
1 NT*	Pass	3 NT	End

* 15–17 points

The play:
West leads ◇3: seven from dummy . . . .
Plan East's defence.

♠: 10 9 5
♡: J 10 3 2
◇: A 7
♣: K Q J 10

♠: J 8 3
♡: A 9 6 5
◇: K J 8
♣: A 7 3

11

♠: A J 4
♡: Q 6 3
◇: A 8 2
♣: A K Q 4

South plays six hearts.

♠: 6 3
♡: A K J 9 8
◇: K J 9 4 3
♣: 6

The play:

a) 1 West leads ♣3, **ace wins**
   2 **Heart to ace,** everybody follows.
      Plan your play. Will it make any difference to you if trumps are 3–2 or 4–1?

b) 1 West leads ♠10, **ace wins**
   2 **Heart to ace,** everybody follows.
      Plan your play. Will it make any difference if trumps are 3–2 or 4–1?

12

♠: Q 8 6 4
♡: 10 5 2
◇: K J 10
♣: Q J 7

♠: K J 5
♡: Q 8 7 4 3
◇: 9 8
♣: A 8 4

Pairs, dealer West
neither side vulnerable.

The bidding:

WEST	NORTH	EAST	SOUTH
Pass	Pass	Pass	1 NT*
Pass	3 NT	End	

*16–18 points

The play:

1 West leads ♡4: two, jack, **ace**
2 South leads ♣3: four, **queen,** five
3 ♣J is led from dummy: *East discards the two of diamonds,*
  South plays the two and **West wins the ace.**

How should West continue?

9. Lucky break or unlucky break.

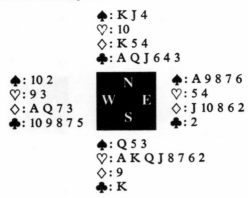

♠: K J 4
♡: 10
◇: K 5 4
♣: A Q J 6 4 3

♠: 10 2
♡: 9 3
◇: A Q 7 3
♣: 10 9 8 7 5

♠: A 9 8 7 6
♡: 5 4
◇: J 10 8 6 2
♣: 2

♠: Q 5 3
♡: A K Q J 8 7 6 2
◇: 9
♣: K

Although the setting of the problem is facetious (only the opponents reach slams off two aces), the point of the hand is worth remembering. At matchpoints, in four hearts, you would want to make the most of a favourable lead to bring in twelve tricks.

The competing lines are to win the king of clubs, cross to dummy with the ten of hearts and lead the ace of clubs, pitching the diamond loser, or to win the ace of clubs and throw the diamond loser at once. Normally both lines will work as only a singleton club can defeat you, but the second line is superior.

The first line gains in the rare situation where either defender has a singleton club and a singleton trump, while the second line caters for a singleton club with East along with one or two trumps. In the actual hand, South wins with dummy's ace of clubs and leads the queen. East ruffs and South over-ruffs. A heart to the ten draws East's last trump and the jack of clubs takes care of the diamond loser.

The principle is easy: adopt the line of play that caters for the less outlandish distribution.

10. Partner's bust stands out

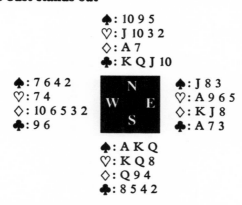

♠ : 10 9 5
♡ : J 10 3 2
◇ : A 7
♣ : K Q J 10

♠ : 7 6 4 2
♡ : 7 4
◇ : 10 6 5 3 2
♣ : 9 6

♠ : J 8 3
♡ : A 9 6 5
◇ : K J 8
♣ : A 7 3

♠ : A K Q
♡ : K Q 8
◇ : Q 9 4
♣ : 8 5 4 2

East should play the jack of diamonds, not the king.

West cannot hold a point, for dummy has 11, East has 13 and South's opening showed 15–17 points (West might have one jack but for the fact that East can see all four of them). The one card of value that West might have is the ten of diamonds.

The lead of ◇3 indicates a four or five-card suit, placing South with at least Q x x in diamonds. East can work out that if he plays the king of diamonds the contract will be bound to succeed, for there will be no entry to the West hand.

But when East plays the jack of diamonds, South will almost surely win with the queen (if he plays low, hold your cards back or learn not to trance for half an hour at trick one). After winning the queen of diamonds South will play a heart or a club. East must win at once and play the *king* of diamonds to dummy's ace. When he regains the lead with his other ace (again taking it at once), he will play his third diamond to give his partner three tricks in the suit.

Note that East must take each ace at the first opportunity (if he ducks even once, declarer can succeed) and he must unblock the king of diamonds. If South began with Q 10 x in diamonds, there was never any defence.

11. Better safe than sorry

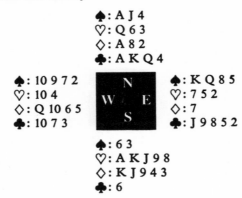

♠: A J 4
♡: Q 6 3
◇: A 8 2
♣: A K Q 4

♠: 10 9 7 2
♡: 10 4
◇: Q 10 6 5
♣: 10 7 3

♠: K Q 8 5
♡: 7 5 2
◇: 7
♣: J 9 8 5 2

♠: 6 3
♡: A K J 9 8
◇: K J 9 4 3
♣: 6

The declarer failed when he played carelessly. He won the ace of clubs, drew trumps, played a spade to the ace, cashed the top clubs and then played ace and another diamond. On the lie of the cards he had to lose two diamond tricks.

a) The correct play is to win ♣A, draw trumps, then play ◇K followed by a low diamond towards the A 8, playing the eight if West plays low. This is a standard safety-play which guards against losing more than one diamond trick.

It makes no difference if trumps are 4–1, as long as the diamonds are tackled before taking discards on the clubs and a diamond is not discarded on the fourth trump.

b) The correct line is to win ♠A, draw trumps, and then play three rounds of clubs, discarding a spade and a diamond, before touching diamonds. If trumps are 3–2, you can continue with ◇K and a low diamond, as in (a), but if trumps are 4–1 you cannot afford to safety-play the diamonds. If East were to capture ◇8 on the second round, a black suit return would finish you. You would have to ruff with your last trump and the diamond suit would be blocked.

12. Blockbuster

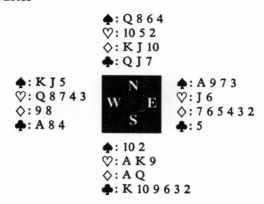

♠: Q 8 6 4
♡: 10 5 2
♢: K J 10
♣: Q J 7

♠: K J 5
♡: Q 8 7 4 3
♢: 9 8
♣: A 8 4

♠: A 9 7 3
♡: J 6
♢: 7 6 5 4 3 2
♣: 5

♠: 10 2
♡: A K 9
♢: A Q
♣: K 10 9 6 3 2

West knows from trick one that South began with ace, king and nine of hearts and from trick three that South began with six clubs. It is off-beat to open one no trump with a six-card suit (although less so at match points). South's shape will almost certainly be 2–3–2–6, and he is known to have two heart tricks and five club tricks. Even without East's ♢2, it is clear that there is no hope of defeating the contract through a diamond switch.

West must switch to spades, leading the jack and playing East to hold A x x x, with the size of those x's being of critical importance. If East holds A 10 9 x, it would be all right to play the king and then the jack. The jack first would also work for that holding, and it is the only card that works on the actual hand.

The ♠5 would block the suit, while the king and then the jack covered by the queen would leave East on lead at the wrong moment. South has no answer to the lead of the jack. If he ducks, West continues with the king and then the five. If the jack is covered by the queen, East wins with the ace, returns the three to the king, and picks up two more spade tricks with his 9 7 over dummy's 8 6.

13

Teams, dealer South,
East-West vulnerable.

The bidding:

SOUTH	WEST	NORTH	EAST
1 NT	Pass	2 ♣	Pass
2 ◇	Pass	3 NT	End

♠: K Q 6 2
♡: A J
◇: 9 7 6 5 2
♣: 8 3

♠: A 5 3
♡: 8 4 2
◇: A 8 4 3
♣: A K J

West leads ♠7. Plan South's play.

14

Teams, dealer North,
both sides vulnerable.

The bidding:

SOUTH	WEST	NORTH	EAST
		1 ◇	Pass
1 ♡	Pass	6 ♡	Double
Pass	Pass	Pass	

You, West, hold:

♠: K 9 7 4
♡: 4
◇: 7 6
♣: A 10 8 7 6 4

What do you lead?

15

Dealer North,
both sides vulnerable.

The bidding:

WEST	NORTH	EAST	SOUTH
	Pass	Pass	1 ♠
Pass	1 NT	Pass	3 ♠
Pass	4 ♠	End	

♠ : J 7
♡ : Q 5 4
◇ : 8 7 6 3 2
♣ : K Q 4

♠ : A K 10 9 4 3
♡ : 8 7 6
◇ : A
♣ : A J 5

The play:
1 West leads ♡10: **East wins the jack**
2 **East wins the king of hearts,** all follow
3 **East wins the ace of hearts,** all follow
4 East leads the queen of diamonds, **South wins the ace.**

How should South continue?

16

Teams, dealer North,
both sides vulnerable.

The bidding:

WEST	NORTH	EAST	SOUTH
	Pass	Pass	1 ♣
Pass	1 ◇	Pass	2 NT
Pass	3 NT	End	

♠ : A J 7
♡ : 4 3 2
◇ : K J 5 3
♣ : J 10 2

♠ : 8 4 3 2
♡ : Q J 7
◇ : 9 8 2
♣ : A 6 3

The play:
1 West leads ♡6: two, jack, **ace**
2 South leads ♠10: five, **ace,** four
3 The ♣J is led from dummy . . . .

Plan East's defence.

13. Keep them guessing

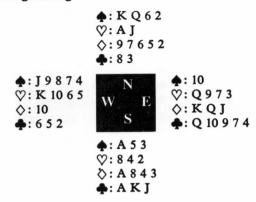

♠: K Q 6 2
♡: A J
◇: 9 7 6 5 2
♣: 8 3

♠: J 9 8 7 4
♡: K 10 6 5
◇: 10
♣: 6 5 2

♠: 10
♡: Q 9 7 3
◇: K Q J
♣: Q 10 9 7 4

♠: A 5 3
♡: 8 4 2
◇: A 8 4 3
♣: A K J

This is merely a matter of setting up some diamond tricks, since you can hardly afford to rely on 3–3 spades and a successful club finesse. But the easier the hand the easier it can be to overlook a precaution.

The correct play is to win the king of spades in dummy (no need to tell East you have the ace) and play a low diamond from both hands. Obviously there will be no problem if diamonds are 2–2, and in this case it makes no difference whether you play the ace on the first round or the second.

But if diamonds are 3–1, the danger is that the defenders may switch to hearts. The advantage of ducking the first round of diamonds is that it gives the defence no chance to signal the heart switch.

At the table the declarer played poorly. He won the first trick with the ace of spades and played ace and another diamond. East, with his finger on the ♣10, changed his mind on seeing his partner's ♣2. He led a heart and the contract went one down.

East might still switch to hearts if left on lead with the first diamond, but you would be unlucky to encounter such a defender. Ninety-nine players out of a hundred would switch to clubs.

14. Bolt of Lightner

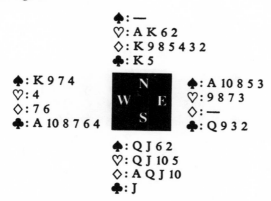

```
                    ♠ : —
                    ♡ : A K 6 2
                    ◇ : K 9 8 5 4 3 2
                    ♣ : K 5
  ♠ : K 9 7 4                        ♠ : A 10 8 5 3
  ♡ : 4                              ♡ : 9 8 7 3
  ◇ : 7 6              W    E        ◇ : —
  ♣ : A 10 8 7 6 4                   ♣ : Q 9 3 2
                    ♠ : Q J 6 2
                    ♡ : Q J 10 5
                    ◇ : A Q J 10
                    ♣ : J
```

The bidding is in the realm of the unreal ('You play a nice game, but I still prefer bridge'), but it occurred in real life in an international match.

The advantage of having specific rules for your Lightner doubles is that it eliminates any ambiguity. Most pairs use Lightner to prohibit the lead of a suit bid by the defence and to ask specifically for the lead of the first non-trump suit bid by dummy.

Here those principles would guide West to a diamond lead in spite of the fact that he has only a doubleton, and that would put the contract two down. The ♣A lead followed by a diamond would put the slam one down, but would be fatal if North's void, marked by his extravagant leap, was in clubs.

At the table East-West's Lightner principles were not defined, merely asking for an unusual lead. West led the ace of clubs, but failed to give credence to his partner's double and continued clubs. That was minus 1660, and a loss of 14 imps when the pair at the other table didn't reach the cold slam in diamonds but stopped in game. The swing was 29 imps, as East-West could have gained 15 imps by defeating six hearts by two tricks.

15. It all adds up

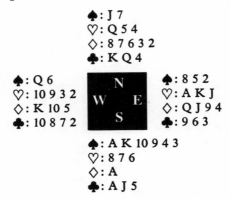

♠: J 7
♡: Q 5 4
◇: 8 7 6 3 2
♣: K Q 4

♠: Q 6
♡: 10 9 3 2
◇: K 10 5
♣: 10 8 7 2

♠: 8 5 2
♡: A K J
◇: Q J 9 4
♣: 9 6 3

♠: A K 10 9 4 3
♡: 8 7 6
◇: A
♣: A J 5

To make the contract South has to avoid losing a trump trick. He should not go wrong, for all the clues to the right play have been paraded in front of him. East has shown up with eight points in hearts and two points in diamonds. For his lead of the queen of diamonds, he almost certainly has the jack of diamonds as well, making a total of eleven points. Since he passed originally, East can hardly have the queen of spades, for that would give him thirteen points and an opening bid.

There is no percentage in taking a finesse that is known to be wrong. South should play the ace and king of spades and hope to drop the queen singleton or doubleton in the West hand. East, of course, would be better advised in future not to give away so much of his hand.

Principle: The right way to play a suit in the abstract may be to finesse, but that is not necessarily the right way to play the whole hand.

16. Second-hand rose

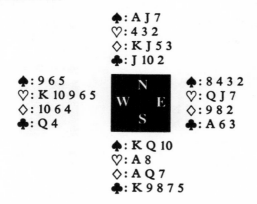

♠: A J 7
♡: 4 3 2
♢: K J 5 3
♣: J 10 2

♠: 9 6 5   **♠: 8 4 3 2**
♡: K 10 9 6 5   **♡: Q J 7**
♢: 10 6 4   **♢: 9 8 2**
♣: Q 4   **♣: A 6 3**

♠: K Q 10
♡: A 8
♢: A Q 7
♣: K 9 8 7 5

East must rise with the ace of clubs and continue hearts to defeat the contract by one trick. If East plays low, South goes up with the king and runs for home with his nine tricks.

How can East tell what to do? Well, if the six of hearts is a normal fourth-highest lead, East can be certain that his partner has the king of hearts. From the Rule of Eleven, East knows that South began with two hearts higher than the six. If these are the ace and king, West must have started with 10 9 8 6 (5), but that is not possible since West would have led the ten from such a holding. Very often *reductio ad absurdum* arguments can point the right way.

South knew, of course, that it was pointless to hold up the ace as the lead of the six of hearts could not be from a six-card suit.

East has a further safeguard. If South really intended to let the jack of clubs run for a finesse, he will probably repeat the finesse later, as a defender will often rise with the ace when holding A Q x.

17

Rubber, dealer North,
both sides vulnerable.

The bidding:

WEST	NORTH	EAST	SOUTH
	Pass	Paŝs	2 ♣
Pass	2 ◇	Pass	2 NT
Pass	3 ♣	Pass	3 NT
Pass	Pass	Pass	

♠: 9 6 4 2
♡: 9 8 3 2
◇: 7
♣: A 10 9 4

```
      N
  W       E
      S
```

♠: A K Q
♡: A K 7
◇: A Q 10
♣: Q 6 3 2

The play:
1 West leads ◇5: seven, jack, **queen.**

Plan South's play.

18

♠: A K J 10 6 3
♡: 7 5
◇: K 4
♣: 8 7 6

♠: 9
♡: K J 9 4
◇: J 7 6 5 2
♣: A J 5

```
      N
  W       E
      S
```

Pairs, dealer South,
both sides vulnerable.

The bidding:

SOUTH	WEST	NORTH	EAST
1 ♣	Pass	1 ♠	Pass
1 NT*	Pass	3 ♠	Pass
3 NT	Pass	Pass	Pass

* 12–14 points

The play:
1 West leads ◇5: **king,** ten, three
2 The ♣6 is led from dummy: four, king . . . .

How should West defend?

19

Teams, dealer West,
neither side vulnerable.

♠: 7 3 2
♡: 8 7 4 3 2
◇: K Q
♣: 9 5 2

The bidding:

WEST	NORTH	EAST	SOUTH
Pass	Pass	Pass	2 ♣
Pass	2 ◇	Pass	3 ♣
Pass	4 ♣	Pass	6 ♣
Pass	Pass	Pass	

♠: A 6 4
♡: A
◇: A J 5
♣: A K J 8 7 4

The play:
1 West leads ♡K: two, five, **ace**
2 **South plays ♣A:** six, two, queen.

How should South continue?

20

Teams, dealer South,
both sides vulnerable.

The bidding:

a)

SOUTH	WEST	NORTH	EAST
1 ◇	1 ♡	3 ◇	3 ♡
6 ◇	Pass	Pass	Double
Pass	Pass	Pass	

b)

SOUTH	WEST	NORTH	EAST
1 ◇	Pass	3 ◇	Pass
6 ◇	Pass	Pass	Double
Pass	Pass	Pass	

In each of the above auctions you are West, holding:

♠: K 10 6
♡: K Q 10 4
◇: 3
♣: 10 6 5 4 2

What do you lead?

17. The whole is greater than the sum of its parts

♠: 9 6 4 2
♡: 9 8 3 2
◇: 7
♣: A 10 9 4

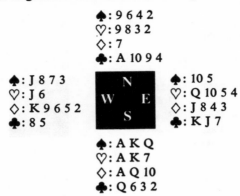

♠: J 8 7 3
♡: J 6
◇: K 9 6 5 2
♣: 8 5

♠: 10 5
♡: Q 10 5 4
◇: J 8 4 3
♣: K J 7

♠: A K Q
♡: A K 7
◇: A Q 10
♣: Q 6 3 2

The best method of playing a suit does not necessarily correspond with the correct way of playing a hand. That's why the mathematician, who knows the best mathematical play in a suit, is not always a competent bridge player. The problems of a whole hand only rarely reduce to the proper handling of a single suit.

Here South needs to establish a second club trick for his contract. In theory the correct way of handling the club holding is to take two finesses, but that would be about the only way to go down on the given hand. The safety of the contract requires that East be kept off lead, so that a second diamond lead does not come through the A 10 until the extra club trick has been established. If a club finesse is taken into the East hand, the diamond return punctures South's tenace and the contract fails ('Unlucky, partner, both clubs were wrong . . .').

Since West is not dangerous on lead, the correct play is a club to the ace and a club back, playing the queen if East follows low. Even if both honours are with West, or if West has K x and East J x x, the contract is safe, for South establishes his ninth trick in clubs before the defenders can get the diamonds going.

18. Chime time

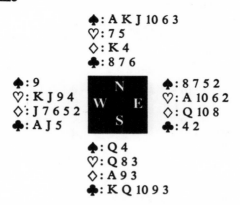

$\spadesuit$: A K J 10 6 3
$\heartsuit$: 7 5
$\diamondsuit$: K 4
$\clubsuit$: 8 7 6

$\spadesuit$: 9
$\heartsuit$: K J 9 4
$\diamondsuit$: J 7 6 5 2
$\clubsuit$: A J 5

$\spadesuit$: 8 7 5 2
$\heartsuit$: A 10 6 2
$\diamondsuit$: Q 10 8
$\clubsuit$: 4 2

$\spadesuit$: Q 4
$\heartsuit$: Q 8 3
$\diamondsuit$: A 9 3
$\clubsuit$: K Q 10 9 3

West should win the ace of clubs and switch to the four of hearts. If West ducks the king of clubs or takes his ace and continues diamonds, the declarer makes nine fast tricks.

West should have heard the bells ringing when South won the diamond lead in dummy and played clubs, not spades. For this play to make any sense, the declarer must have the queen of spades. Otherwise he would win the diamond lead in hand with the ace and attack spades, retaining the $\diamondsuit$K in dummy as an entry for the established spades.

If South has $\spadesuit$Q, he can be counted for eight tricks (six spades and two diamonds), and it is long odds that he has the $\clubsuit$Q along with the king. That means he is home as soon as he regains the lead.

All the evidence underlines the urgent need for a heart switch, but many defenders would mechanically continue diamonds, reassured by East's $\diamondsuit$10 at trick one. East must encourage diamonds, of course, since for all he knows West may have the ace.

19. From tyro to maestro

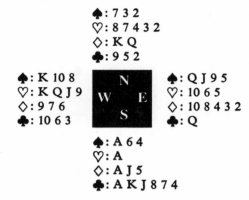

♠: 7 3 2
♡: 8 7 4 3 2
♢: K Q
♣: 9 5 2

♠: K 10 8
♡: K Q J 9
♢: 9 7 6
♣: 10 6 3

♠: Q J 9 5
♡: 10 6 5
♢: 10 8 4 3 2
♣: Q

♠: A 6 4
♡: A
♢: A J 5
♣: A K J 8 7 4

The fall of the ♣Q simplifies the problem, but the best line applies whether the queen appears or not.

The novice draws three rounds of trumps and remains saddled with two spade losers.

The moderate player draws a second round of trumps ('just to check that the queen was singleton, partner'), then plays three rounds of diamonds to discard a spade from dummy. Next comes ace and another spade, but West wins and plays a third round of trumps, leaving South with a second spade loser.

The competent player does not draw a second round of trumps. He plays three rounds of diamonds, pitching a spade from dummy, then ace and another spade, and eventually ruffs his third spade in dummy.

The expert plays a low spade from both hands at trick three. He wins the return, discards dummy's second spade on the third diamond, plays ♠A, ruffs his third spade and draws the outstanding trumps.

Why does the expert adopt this line? Because the approach of the competent player attracts an unnecessary risk. After three rounds of diamonds and the ace and another spade, East can win and play a fourth diamond, promoting a trump trick for West. There is no such risk attached to the expert's line.

Well, which category did you achieve?

20. Lightner strikes twice

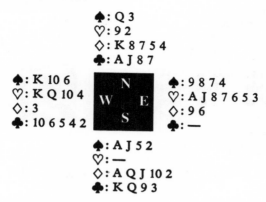

♠: Q 3
♥: 9 2
♦: K 8 7 5 4
♣: A J 8 7

♠: K 10 6   ♠: 9 8 7 4
♥: K Q 10 4   ♥: A J 8 7 6 5 3
♦: 3   ♦: 9 6
♣: 10 6 5 4 2   ♣: —

♠: A J 5 2
♥: —
♦: A Q J 10 2
♣: K Q 9 3

Do you think the auctions are unusual? They happened in an international match. Do you think that after the Lightner double calling for an unusual lead no West could consider leading the king of hearts?. Both Wests led ♡K and both declarers scored 1540. Flat board!

The double of a freely-bid slam usually indicates a void in the doubler's hand, and it asks his partner to make an unusual lead. If dummy has bid a suit other than trumps, the double asks for a lead of that suit. If dummy has bid nothing but the trump suit, the double acts in a negative sense, prohibiting the lead of a trump and the lead of any suit bid by the defenders.

In auction (a) the double specifically asks West not to lead a heart, and West should realize that his partner's void is more likely to be in clubs than in spades. In auction (b) it is more difficult, but again the void is most likely to be opposite the long suit.

West should lead a club, preferably a middle club, since he cannot tell, before seeing dummy, whether he wants a heart or a spade return. It is better not to lead a card which might give his partner suit-preference ideas. On this hand it wouldn't matter, for West must always come to his spade trick.

21

Teams, dealer West,
both sides vulnerable.

♠: J
♡: K
◇: J 7 4 3 2
♣: A K 9 8 4 2

The bidding:

SOUTH	WEST	NORTH	EAST
	Pass	Pass	Pass
1 ♠	Pass	2 ♣	Pass
2 ♠	Pass	3 ◇	Pass
3 NT	Pass	Pass	Pass

♠: A 6 4 3 2
♡: A 9 8
◇: A 8
♣: 10 6 3

The play:
1 West leads ♡5: **king,** six, eight.

How should declarer continue?

22

Teams, dealer East,
North-South vulnerable.

♠: Q J 10 7 4
♡: A
◇: 7 6 5 3 2
♣: Q 5

The bidding:

WEST	NORTH	EAST	SOUTH
		Pass	2 ♡*
Pass	2 ♠**	Pass	2 NT
Pass	3 ◇	Pass	3 NT
Pass	Pass	Pass	

♠: A 9 8 6 3
♡: 7 6 5
◇: K 9
♣: 10 6 4

* Natural, strong, one-round force
** Natural, positive response, game-force

The play:
1 West leads ♣7: **queen,** six, two
2 The ♠4 is led from dummy . . . .

Plan East's defence.

23

Teams, dealer North,
both sides vulnerable.

The bidding:

WEST	NORTH	EAST	SOUTH
	1 ♡	Pass	2 ◇
Pass	3 ♡	Pass	3 NT
Pass	4 ◇	Pass	6 ◇
Pass	Pass	Pass	

♠ : J
♡ : A K J 8 7 6 5
◇ : K 9 5
♣ : A Q

♠ : Q 8 4 3
♡ : —
◇ : A Q J 6 4 3
♣ : K 7 2

The play:
1 **West leads ♠K:** jack, five, three
2 West leads ♠2 . . . .

How should South play?

24

Rubber, dealer South,
North-South vulnerable.

The bidding:

SOUTH	WEST	NORTH	EAST
1 ♡*	4 ◇	4 ♡**	End

 * 5-card suit
** Succumbing to pressure

♠ : A 9 8 5 2
♡ : 10 6
◇ : A 9
♣ : 10 6 5 3

♠ : J 7 3
♡ : Q J 9 4
◇ : Q 3
♣ : 9 7 4 2

The play:
1 West leads ♣J: three, two, **ace**
2 **South plays ♡A:** three, six, four
3 **South plays ♡K:** eight, ten, nine
4 South plays ♡2: *West discards ◇8*, declarer looks annoyed, a spade is
  pitched from dummy and **East wins ♡J**
5 **East leads ◇Q:** four, two, nine.

How should East continue?

21. Category mistake

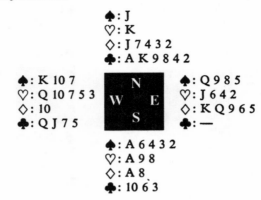

♠ : J
♡ : K
◇ : J 7 4 3 2
♣ : A K 9 8 4 2

♠ : K 10 7
♡ : Q 10 7 5 3
◇ : 10
♣ : Q J 7 5

N
W   E
S

♠ : Q 9 8 5
♡ : J 6 4 2
◇ : K Q 9 6 5
♣ : —

♠ : A 6 4 3 2
♡ : A 9 8
◇ : A 8
♣ : 10 6 3

The poor player continues with the ace and king of clubs, and even if he remembers to unblock the ten of clubs he will succeed only 40% of the time. He will fail whenever clubs are 3–1 or 4–0.

The average player wins the ♡K and then plays the ace of clubs and a low club. He thus caters for any 2–2 or 3–1 break. But if the hand is as shown above his play will fail, for West will play low on the second round of clubs and the declarer will be left with only three club tricks.

Through bitter experience, the top player knows that the right play after winning the king of hearts is to lead a low club from dummy at once. This is a 95% play, succeeding in every position except when East has all four clubs. If West ducks the ten of clubs on the above hand, declarer can make an overtrick by taking a double club finesse.

22. Rise and shine

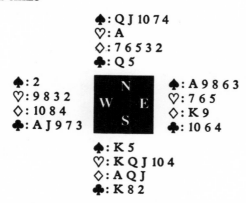

♠: Q J 10 7 4
♡: A
♢: 7 6 5 3 2
♣: Q 5

♠: 2
♡: 9 8 3 2
♢: 10 8 4
♣: A J 9 7 3

♠: A 9 8 6 3
♡: 7 6 5
♢: K 9
♣: 10 6 4

♠: K 5
♡: K Q J 10 4
♢: A Q J
♣: K 8 2

East should rise with the ace of spades and return a club, setting the contract one trick.

In view of South's strong opening and the strength in dummy, the defence cannot hope to prevail by the passive approach of ducking the first spade and thus limiting the declarer to three spade tricks. Unless the clubs can be run, it is unlikely that the defence can come to five tricks.

The hand arose between the Aces and France in the 1971 Bermuda Bowl. Wolff, East, correctly rose with ♠A and returned a club to defeat three no trumps. The same contract was made in the other room when the declarer took the diamond finesse at trick two, making five heart tricks, three diamonds and a club.

There is not much to choose between the lines adopted by the two declarers, each depending essentially on a key honour being well-placed, although playing spades has the added advantage of capitalizing on a possible 4–4 club break. Note that if East ducks the first spade the declarer will certainly make his contract by crossing to the ace of hearts and taking the diamond finesse.

23. It only rains when you forget your umbrella

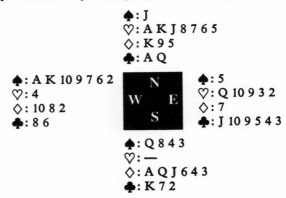

♠: J
♡: A K J 8 7 6 5
◇: K 9 5
♣: A Q

♠: A K 10 9 7 6 2
♡: 4
◇: 10 8 2
♣: 8 6

♠: 5
♡: Q 10 9 3 2
◇: 7
♣: J 10 9 5 4 3

♠: Q 8 4 3
♡: —
◇: A Q J 6 4 3
♣: K 7 2

It seems safe enough to let the spade run round to your queen. Surely West has not plucked the ♠K lead out of thin air. Oh well, it cannot cost to ruff in dummy.

Once you have reached that conclusion, it is obvious that you should ruff with the nine of diamonds. At the table the declarer carelessly ruffed with the ◇5. East quickly over-ruffed before South could change his mind, and that was one down.

On the actual hand it would work just as well to ruff with ◇K, but that could cost if diamonds were 4–0, a 10% chance, much greater than the likelihood of a 7–1 spade break.

West could have made it harder by starting with ♠A rather than the king, but the ruff with ◇9 would still be correct. It is the sort of careful play that will usually prove unnecessary but will occasionally pay a big dividend.

24. Don't hang on ... for dear life

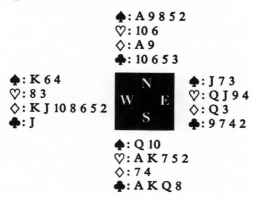

♠: A 9 8 5 2
♡: 10 6
◊: A 9
♣: 10 6 5 3

♠: K 6 4
♡: 8 3
◊: K J 10 8 6 5 2
♣: J

♠: J 7 3
♡: Q J 9 4
◊: Q 3
♣: 9 7 4 2

♠: Q 10
♡: A K 7 5 2
◊: 7 4
♣: A K Q 8

When the queen of diamonds is allowed to hold, you must cash your top trump before continuing with a second diamond. You should assume West's ♣J lead to be a singleton (few competent players lead from J x unless partner has bid the suit), so South is known to have started with five hearts, four clubs, two diamonds (why else would he duck the diamond?) and hence two spades (without the king if you are to have a chance).

If you fail to cash your top heart but play another diamond, declarer will take the ace, play off the clubs and then throw you in with the heart. You will have to lead a spade and if South guesses right, inserting the ten, he will make his contract (he should guess right, for if you held ♠K West should have overtaken ◊Q in order to play a spade).

Why did South look annoyed? Because he realized, a second too late, that he had missed a chance. After two rounds of hearts he should have switched, taking the better chance of the double spade finesse to eliminate the diamond loser. The hearts were unlikely to be 3–3.

South will be even more annoyed when his partner points out (as partners always do) that he missed a second opportunity. If South wins the first diamond, eliminates the clubs, and plays another diamond, he can always force you to lead a spade in the end-game.

Part two Intermediate level

A competent player should score at least 75% in this section and should not require more than three or four minutes to come up with the winning line for each problem. A strong player should score 90%.

25

Rubber, dealer East,
East-West vulnerable.

The bidding:

WEST	NORTH	EAST	SOUTH
		Pass	1 ♠
Pass	2 ♣	Pass	3 ♣
Pass	3 ♠	Pass	4 ♠
Pass	Pass	Pass	

♠ : 8 3 2
♡ : Q 6
◇ : 9 8 6 4
♣ : A K J 9

♠ : A 7 6 5 4
♡ : A 5 3
◇ : A
♣ : Q 8 6 4

The play:
West leads ♠K : two, nine . . .

Plan South's play.

26

Rubber, dealer South,
neither side vulnerable.

The bidding:

SOUTH	WEST	NORTH	EAST
2 NT*	Pass	3 NT	End

* 21–23 points

♠ : Q 8 7
♡ : 7 5 4
◇ : J 8 7 2
♣ : Q 9 3

♠ : K 9 5
♡ : A Q J 6
◇ : 9 5 4
♣ : 8 6 2

The play:
1 West leads ♠J : seven, five, **ace**
2 South leads ◇Q : **king**, two, four
3 West leads ♠10 : queen, **king**, two.

How should East continue ?

27

Dealer East,
both sides vulnerable.

The bidding:

WEST	NORTH	EAST	SOUTH
		Pass	1 NT
Pass	3 NT	End	

♠: Q 6 5
♡: 6 4
◇: A Q 6 5 3
♣: A 4 3

♠: A K J 10
♡: A 5 2
◇: 7 4 2
♣: J 8 7

The play:
1 West leads ♡3, East plays the king.

How should South play?

28

Dealer North,
East-West vulnerable.

The bidding:

WEST	NORTH	EAST	SOUTH
	1 ◇	Pass	1 ♠
2 ♡	3 ◇	Pass	6 ♠
Pass	Pass	Pass	

♠: 6
♡: K 8 3
◇: A K 10 9 8 5 3
♣: Q 4

♠: 9 5 4
♡: J 7 6
◇: Q 7 4 2
♣: K 7 2

The play:
1 West leads ♣5: queen, king, **ace**
2 **South plays ♠A:** seven, six, five
3 **South plays ♠K:** queen, ♡3, ♠4
4 **South plays ♠J:** *West discards ♡10 and dummy throws ◇3*
5 South leads ◇J: *West discards ♡2, dummy plays low . . . .*

How should East defend?

25. Ask little, receive much

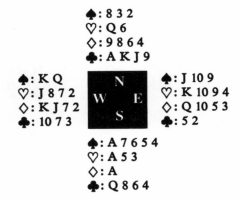

```
                    ♠: 8 3 2
                    ♡: Q 6
                    ◇: 9 8 6 4
                    ♣: A K J 9
♠: K Q                  N           ♠: J 10 9
♡: J 8 7 2         W         E      ♡: K 10 9 4
◇: K J 7 2                          ◇: Q 10 5 3
♣: 10 7 3               S           ♣: 5 2
                    ♠: A 7 6 5 4
                    ♡: A 5 3
                    ◇: A
                    ♣: Q 8 6 4
```

The combination of bidding and lead should make you confident that trumps are splitting 3–2. A defender with K Q J 10 in trumps can rarely refrain from doubling.

The novice wins the first spade, succeeding if West holds the king of hearts, but failing in most layouts when the heart king is wrong since the defenders will clear trumps. Winning the first spade succeeds on the actual hand because the trumps are blocked, but that is fortuitous.

The good player ducks the first spade, wins the second and leads a heart. He will succeed if West has the king of hearts or if East has the king without the last trump. He will make four spades in most situations, but not on the actual hand.

The expert succeeds whenever trumps are 3–2 regardless of the location of the king of hearts. He wins the second spade and plays ◇A, club to ace, diamond ruff, club to king, diamond ruff, club to jack, diamond ruff. If a defender ruffs at any time, dummy has a trump left to take care of declarer's last heart. If the master trump is still at large, South continues with ♣Q. If this is ruffed, the declarer still makes the ♡A and a heart ruff (on the actual hand he makes eleven tricks, for East has to lead away from ♡K). If the queen of clubs is not ruffed, declarer just cashes ♡A as his tenth trick.

26. Hold your horses

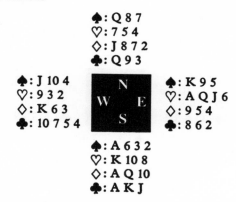

♠: Q 8 7
♡: 7 5 4
◇: J 8 7 2
♣: Q 9 3

♠: J 10 4
♡: 9 3 2
◇: K 6 3
♣: 10 7 5 4

♠: K 9 5
♡: A Q J 6
◇: 9 5 4
♣: 8 6 2

♠: A 6 3 2
♡: K 10 8
◇: A Q 10
♣: A K J

East must switch at once to hearts in order to establish a fifth trick for the defence.

At the table East cashed the nine of spades and then led the queen of hearts. The declarer played the king and had nine tricks by virtue of the thirteenth spade.

Once West has shown up with ♠J and ◇K, South is marked with all the remaining high cards for his opening bid. East should realize that his partner has led from a short suit. The lead of the jack is standard from J 10 9 x or J 10 8 x (neither of which are possible here) and from J 10 x. But from J 10 x x the fourth-highest would be normal. If East appreciates that West has made a short suit lead, he will not be tempted to cash the nine of spades since that can help only the declarer.

The heart switch is needed to set up an additional heart winner while the spade control is still held. If declarer is able to run for home with one spade, one heart, three diamonds and four clubs, there was nothing you could have done.

27. A psychological edge

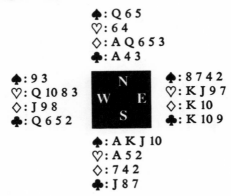

                    ♠ : Q 6 5
                    ♡ : 6 4
                    ◇ : A Q 6 5 3
                    ♣ : A 4 3

♠ : 9 3   ♠ : 8 7 4 2
♡ : Q 10 8 3   ♡ : K J 9 7
◇ : J 9 8   ◇ : K 10
♣ : Q 6 5 2   ♣ : K 10 9

                    ♠ : A K J 10
                    ♡ : A 5 2
                    ◇ : 7 4 2
                    ♣ : J 8 7

In practice the declarer failed when he held up the ace of hearts until
the third round and then played a diamond to the queen and king.

The correct play at trick one is the ace of hearts. The opening lead is
likely to be an honest fourth-highest card, which means that the hearts
will be 4–4. It would be unfortunate (partner might have a stronger word
for it) if you ducked the heart and East returned a club in a situation
where the contract could have been made by taking the ace of hearts at
once and tackling the diamonds.

To make your contract you will need to bring in the diamond suit. The
'natural' play is to finesse the queen, but on the given layout this fails.
The best approach is the psychological one which does nothing to
jeopardize your genuine chances: cross to ♠Q and lead a low diamond
from dummy. East may well think that you have the jack and go up with
the king, ending your problems. Alternatively he may give away the
position by trancing before playing low.

If East plays low smoothly, you can later take the normal finesse of the
queen. The first-round finesse works 50% of the time. The delayed
finesse works 50% plus the occasions when East with king doubleton
goes wrong. It is a something-for-nothing play.

28. Accepting Greek gifts

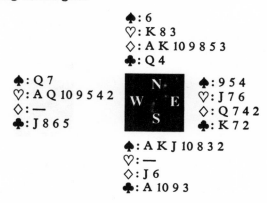

♠ : 6
♡ : K 8 3
◇ : A K 10 9 8 5 3
♣ : Q 4

♠ : Q 7
♡ : A Q 10 9 5 4 2
◇ : —
♣ : J 8 6 5

♠ : 9 5 4
♡ : J 7 6
◇ : Q 7 4 2
♣ : K 7 2

♠ : A K J 10 8 3 2
♡ : —
◇ : J 6
♣ : A 10 9 3

East should win the queen of diamonds at once and return a club.
How does East know to return a club and not a heart? Well, it helps to know the calibre of the opposition, of course, but surely no sane South would have jumped to six spades, missing the queen of trumps, the top diamonds and the king and queen of clubs, if he also had a heart loser. There is, after all, a convention known as Blackwood.

In general it is good advice to beware of Greek gifts, and many players would duck the first diamond in order to shut out dummy's suit. But in this case the declarer does not need more than three tricks from the diamonds. If East ducks, South continues with the ace and king of diamonds, pitching a club, and then concedes a club to the jack. The duck gives him the chance to recover from his wrong guess at trick one and provides him with a story to tell for weeks to come.

East should realize that the fate of the contract depends on the location of the jack of clubs. If South has it, he is bound to make twelve tricks whether the first diamond is ducked or not.

29

Rubber bridge, dealer North,
neither side vulnerable,
North-South have a part-score of 60.

♠: 10 6 2
♡: 9 8 7 3
◇: K 5
♣: A Q 6 2

The bidding:

WEST	NORTH	EAST	SOUTH
	Pass	Pass	1 ♡
Pass	2 ♡	2 ♠	3 ♡
Pass	Pass	Pass	

♠: Q 7
♡: A K J 10 6
◇: Q 10 3
♣: J 5 4

The play:
1 West leads the ♠5: two, **king**, seven
2 **East cashes ♠A:** queen, eight, six
3 East leads ♡5: **ace,** four, three
4 South plays ◇3 to the **king,** which wins.

How should South continue?

30

Teams, dealer North,
both sides vulnerable.

♠: Q 4
♡: 10 9 8 7 5
◇: A Q 10 6 2
♣: 7

The bidding:

WEST	NORTH	EAST	SOUTH
	Pass	1 ♠	2 ♡
4 ♠	5 ♡	5 ♠	Pass
Pass	6 ♡	Double	End

♠: K J 10 8 6 2
♡: A 3
◇: —
♣: K J 8 4 3

West leads ♠A. Plan East's defence.

31

Rubber, dealer West,
neither side vulnerable.

The bidding:

WEST	NORTH	EAST	SOUTH
3 ♣	Pass	Pass	3 ♡
Pass	4 ♡	End	

♠: K 10 9 5 2
♡: K 4
◇: 10 7 6 4 2
♣: 5

♠: A 7 3
♡: A Q J 9 6 5
◇: 3
♣: J 10 3

The play:
1 **West leads ♣K:** five, two, three
2 West switches to ♡3.

Plan South's play.

32

Rubber, dealer North,
neither side vulnerable.

The bidding:

WEST	NORTH	EAST	SOUTH
	1 ♡	2 ◇	2 ♠
Pass	3 ♣	Pass	3 ♠
Pass	3 NT	Pass	4 ♠
Pass	Pass	Pass	

♠: 2
♡: A Q 7 5 3
◇: K 8 5
♣: A K J 3

♠: A 3
♡: K 10 9 8
◇: Q J 9 7 6 2
♣: 9

The play:
1 **West leads ◇A:** five, queen, four
2 West leads ◇3: **king,** two, ten
3 The ♠2 is led from dummy . . . .

How should East defend?

29. All in good time

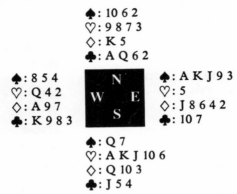

♠: 10 6 2
♡: 9 8 7 3
♢: K 5
♣: A Q 6 2

♠: 8 5 4
♡: Q 4 2
♢: A 9 7
♣: K 9 8 3

♠: A K J 9 3
♡: 5
♢: J 8 6 4 2
♣: 10 7

♠: Q 7
♡: A K J 10 6
♢: Q 10 3
♣: J 5 4

The declarer failed in practice when he played a trump from dummy at trick five. He won the king of hearts, took the club finesse and played a diamond to the ten and ace, but West simply cashed the queen of hearts and exited with a spade (a diamond would have done as well), leaving South with a club loser for one down.

Declarer mistimed his play. If the hearts are 2–2, there is no urgency about drawing the second round. Best at trick five is to return a diamond to the ten and ace. South can ruff the spade return, lead a low club to the queen, a heart to the king, then cash the queen of diamonds and throw West in with the heart to lead away from his king of clubs. It would not matter if West held an extra diamond or spade instead of his fourth club, for he would then have an unenviable choice between leading away from the king of clubs and conceding a ruff and discard.

South can also succeed if West has the jack of diamonds as well as the ace, provided that West has no more than three cards in both spades and diamonds.

30. Sledgehammer produces cracking results

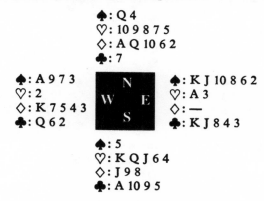

♠: Q 4
♡: 10 9 8 7 5
♢: A Q 10 6 2
♣: 7

♠: A 9 7 3
♡: 2
♢: K 7 5 4 3
♣: Q 6 2

♠: K J 10 8 6 2
♡: A 3
♢: —
♣: K J 8 4 3

♠: 5
♡: K Q J 6 4
♢: J 9 8
♣: A 10 9 5

Six spades goes down only if they find the club ruff, but that does not mean you should settle for less than the maximum penalty from North-South. Obviously you want partner to give you a diamond ruff, but how can you focus his attention on the diamonds ?

A high spade would merely request a spade continuation. Some partnerships arrange that a high-spot card asks for a continuation, while an honour indicates suit-preference, but for most partnerships the ♠J would merely be a command to continue spades. A low spade would ask for a switch, but would partner find the right switch ?

At the table, East played ♠2 at trick one. West reasoned that, in view of his own diamond holding, East was unlikely to want a diamond. The club switch allowed declarer to escape for one down.

The dramatic card, and the right card to play at trick one, is ♠K—an impossible card in any natural sense. If partner now doesn't work out that a diamond switch is required, it's time to invest in a new partner.

Isn't it dangerous to play the ♠K ? If declarer ruffs the first trick you will have set up ♠Q as a winner. Even so, it is unlikely that the ♠Q will provide South with a useful discard. Any missing diamond honours are onside, and South can hardly hold a singleton club loser.

31. Duck for dinner

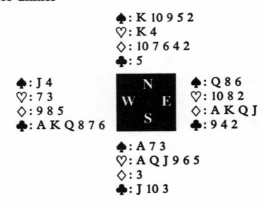

$\spadesuit$: K 10 9 5 2
$\heartsuit$: K 4
$\diamondsuit$: 10 7 6 4 2
$\clubsuit$: 5

$\spadesuit$: J 4
$\heartsuit$: 7 3
$\diamondsuit$: 9 8 5
$\clubsuit$: A K Q 8 7 6

$\spadesuit$: Q 8 6
$\heartsuit$: 10 8 2
$\diamondsuit$: A K Q J
$\clubsuit$: 9 4 2

$\spadesuit$: A 7 3
$\heartsuit$: A Q J 9 6 5
$\diamondsuit$: 3
$\clubsuit$: J 10 3

But for that annoying trump switch you might have been able to ruff both remaining club losers in dummy.

The worst way of tackling the hand would be to draw the rest of the trumps immediately. You would then succeed only on some miraculous spade position, for if you lost a spade trick the opponents would cash a diamond and two further clubs for two down.

A slight improvement would be to ruff a club in dummy, return to $\spadesuit$A, draw trumps and then duck a spade. That could work if East won the spade and had no more clubs, or if the defenders tried to cash diamonds instead of clubs.

But the best chance is to bank on 3–2 spades and duck a spade at trick three. No matter in which hand the trick is won, the defenders are helpless. As soon as you regain the lead you can draw trumps and run the spades for ten tricks. The key is to leave the second trump in dummy to control the club suit while you go about establishing the spades.

If the spades turn out to be 4–1 and someone gets a ruff, console yourself with the reflection that you couldn't make the contract anyway.

32. Fools rush in

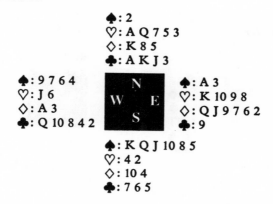

```
                    ♠ : 2
                    ♡ : A Q 7 5 3
                    ◇ : K 8 5
                    ♣ : A K J 3
    ♠ : 9 7 6 4           ┌───────┐           ♠ : A 3
    ♡ : J 6               │   N   │           ♡ : K 10 9 8
    ◇ : A 3               │ W   E │           ◇ : Q J 9 7 6 2
    ♣ : Q 10 8 4 2        │   S   │           ♣ : 9
                          └───────┘
                    ♠ : K Q J 10 8 5
                    ♡ : 4 2
                    ◇ : 10 4
                    ♣ : 7 6 5
```

The best defence is to duck the spade lead from dummy, win the next spade with the ace and play a diamond, hoping to promote a trump trick for partner. The setting trick may then come from hearts.

The trouble with playing the ace on the first round is that it will collect a small card, not an honour, from South, making a trump promotion less likely. Of course, even if you duck the first spade, South can, in theory, thwart your plans by continuing with a low spade to knock out your ace. If he does this in practice, try holding your cards closer to your chest.

There is no layout where it can be right to rush in with the ♠A at once. Even in the unlikely event of South having eight spades to the K J 10 and West Q x, rising with the ace and playing a diamond can achieve no more than preventing the overtrick. South must always make six spade tricks to add to the four high-card tricks in dummy.

33

Pairs, dealer North
neither side vulnerable.

♠: A 8 6 2
♡: A 9 8 5 2
◇: A 4
♣: Q 2

The bidding:

WEST	NORTH	EAST	SOUTH
	1 ♡	Pass	2 ♣
Pass	2 ♡	Pass	2 ♠
Pass	4 ♠	Pass	4 NT
Pass	5 ♠	Pass	6 ♣
Pass	Pass	Double	End

♠: Q J 7 4
♡: 3
◇: 5
♣: A K J 10 9 4 3

The play:
1 West leads ♡Q: **ace,** seven, three.

How should South plan the play?

34

♠: A 8 2
♡: J 3
◇: J 10 7 3
♣: K 8 4 3

♠: Q 9 7 4 3
♡: 10 6 5 4
◇: 8 4
♣: J 2

Pairs, dealer South,
North-South vulnerable.

The bidding:

SOUTH	WEST	NORTH	EAST
1 NT*	Pass	2 ♣**	Pass
2 NT***	Pass	3 NT	End

    * 14–17 points
    ** Extended Stayman
    *** 16–17, no four-card major

The play:
1 West leads ♠4: two, **king,** ten
2 East returns ♠6: jack, **queen,** eight.

How should West continue?

35

Dealer East,
neither side vulnerable.

♠: 5 3 2
♡: Q 6
◇: 7 3 2
♣: 10 7 6 5 3

The bidding:

WEST	NORTH	EAST	SOUTH
		1 NT*	Double
Pass	2 ♣	Pass	4 ♠
Pass	Pass	Pass	

* 12–14 points

♠: K Q J 10 4
♡: A K
◇: A K J 4
♣: K J

West leads the ten of hearts.

1 Calm down. Until the hand is over, forget about partner removing the
  biggest penalty double you ever had against the weak no trump.
  You win the ace of hearts
2 You lead ♠K: **East wins the ace**
3 East returns ♠7: **queen,** eight, three.

Plan the play.

36

♠: J 8 4 2
♡: J 8 5 4
◇: K Q 7
♣: 6 2

♠: 9 6 3
♡: K 10 6
◇: 6 4 3 2
♣: K Q J

Dealer South,
North-South vulnerable.

The bidding:

SOUTH	WEST	NORTH	EAST
1 ♣	Pass	1 ♡	Pass
3 NT	Pass	Pass	Pass

The play:
1 West leads ♣K: two, three, **ace**
2 South returns ♣10: **jack,** six, seven.

How should West continue ?

33. En garde

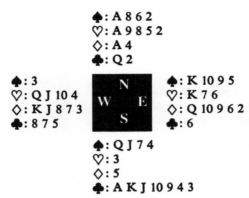

♠: A 8 6 2
♡: A 9 8 5 2
◇: A 4
♣: Q 2

♠: 3
♡: Q J 10 4
◇: K J 8 7 3
♣: 8 7 5

♠: K 10 9 5
♡: K 7 6
◇: Q 10 9 6 2
♣: 6

♠: Q J 7 4
♡: 3
◇: 5
♣: A K J 10 9 4 3

In view of the double the trumps are sure to be stacked on your right, and you must hope they are no worse than 4–1. After ♡A, lead a low spade to your queen, return to dummy with ◇A and lead another low spade to your jack. If East ducks twice, continue with a third spade to the ace and then run the clubs.

Should East rise with ♠K on the second round and force you to ruff, play off the jack of spades, cross to dummy with ♣Q and draw the last trump before running the clubs.

The trap to avoid is playing the ♠A early. To start with the ace and another spade, or with a spade to the queen and a spade back to the ace, is to court disaster. East will play the king on the next trump lead and return a heart, forcing you to ruff with an honour, and the hand will explode in your face.

Even without the double, you should tackle the trump suit in the same way. It would be greedy to try for an overtrick by running the jack or queen, playing for the remote chance of finding East with 10 9 doubleton.

34. Asleep at the wheel

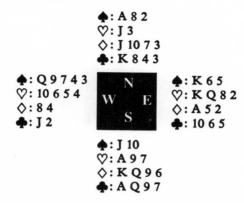

♠: A 8 2
♡: J 3
◇: J 10 7 3
♣: K 8 4 3

♠: Q 9 7 4 3
♡: 10 6 5 4
◇: 8 4
♣: J 2

♠: K 6 5
♡: K Q 8 2
◇: A 5 2
♣: 10 6 5

♠: J 10
♡: A 9 7
◇: K Q 9 6
♣: A Q 9 7

At the table a normally competent West fell asleep and continued with a third spade. The declarer won, and had nine tricks after knocking out the ace of diamonds.

With no entry for his spades, West should not persevere with the suit but should switch, naturally to hearts as declarer has denied holding four hearts. From West's point of view the heart switch may or may not break the contract. A spade continuation certainly won't. Even if the bidding had been less illuminating (1 NT, 2 NT; 3 NT, for example), the heart switch would still be right.

It is true that East could have protected himself against a sleepy partner by switching to the king of hearts at trick two. Perhaps he should have done so, for this is the only successful defence if West's spades are headed by the jack instead of the queen. But on the actual hand the spade continuation should have worked out well when West was allowed to win the second trick. By switching to hearts at this point, West could have defeated the contract by two tricks for a top score.

35. Partly by elimination

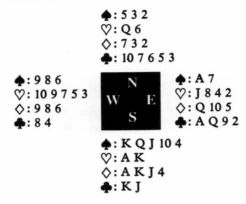

♠ : 5 3 2
♡ : Q 6
◇ : 7 3 2
♣ : 10 7 6 5 3

♠ : 9 8 6
♡ : 10 9 7 5 3
◇ : 9 8 6
♣ : 8 4

♠ : A 7
♡ : J 8 4 2
◇ : Q 10 5
♣ : A Q 9 2

♠ : K Q J 10 4
♡ : A K
◇ : A K J 4
♣ : K J

Trap 1: You must not draw the third round of trumps at this point. If diamonds are 4–2, you will need to ruff the fourth round of diamonds in dummy, although to do this you may have to depend on a defensive error (for example, if East began with Q x in diamonds and three spades he should not ruff the jack of diamonds but wait to over-ruff dummy).

If diamonds are 3–3, it is still essential not to draw the outstanding trump immediately.

Trap 2: You must cash the king of hearts before playing the third round of diamonds. On the actual hand East is put on lead with the third diamond and he must either open up the clubs or give you a ruff and discard by returning a heart. That is why dummy needs to retain a trump, to enable you to produce a partial elimination. This way you lose only one trump, one diamond and one club. But if you fail to eliminate the hearts, East has an easy exit and you will eventually have to lose two club tricks.

36. Your strength is their weakness

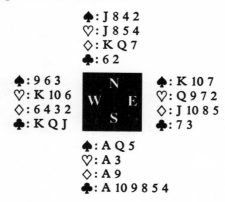

♠: J 8 4 2
♡: J 8 5 4
◇: K Q 7
♣: 6 2

♠: 9 6 3
♡: K 10 6
◇: 6 4 3 2
♣: K Q J

♠: K 10 7
♡: Q 9 7 2
◇: J 10 8 5
♣: 7 3

♠: A Q 5
♡: A 3
◇: A 9
♣: A 10 9 8 5 4

Clearly West has to find a switch, and a heart switch looks the most promising shot in view of the weakness of dummy's holding. When dummy has bid a suit, declarers tend to rely on the suit being sufficiently held for no trump purposes. If dummy goes down with a weak holding in his suit, therefore, it is often a good idea for the defenders to switch to that suit.

Once West has decided to switch to hearts there remains the question of which card to lead. The defenders need three heart tricks, and West should bear in mind the need to unblock. The correct choice is the ten, which is the only card to defeat the contract in the actual hand. South wins with the ace and plays another club. West wins and plays king and another heart to finish South off.

Note that South can succeed if West starts with either the king or the six of hearts. But the lead of the heart ten leaves him without any answer.

37

Dealer North,
neither side vulnerable.

The bidding:

WEST	NORTH	EAST	SOUTH
	Pass	1 ♣	Pass
1 ♢	Double	1 NT*	2 ♠
3 ♣	4 ♠	Double	End

* 12–15 points

♠: K 7 6 3 2
♡: A J 10 7 6
♢: Q 10 4
♣: —

♠: Q 9 8 4
♡: K 4 2
♢: 7 6
♣: K J 5 3

The play:
1 West leads ♣A: *ruffed in dummy*, East plays the two
2 ♠2 is led from dummy: ten, **queen,** five.

How should South continue?

38

Dealer South,
North-South vulnerable.

The bidding:

SOUTH	WEST	NORTH	EAST
1 ♠*	4 ♢	4 ♠	Double
Pass	Pass	Pass	

* North-South do not open 4-card majors.

♠: J 8 7 5
♡: 7 4 3
♢: A K
♣: Q 8 6 2

♠: A Q 3
♡: A 8
♢: 7 4 3
♣: A J 10 5 3

The play:
1 West leads ♢2: **ace,** three, ten
2 ♠5 is played from dummy . . . .

How should East defend?

39

Teams, dealer North,
both sides vulnerable.

The bidding:

SOUTH	WEST	NORTH	EAST
		Pass	Pass
1 ♡	1 ♠	3 ♡*	Pass
4 ♡	Pass	Pass	Pass

* North-South play 5-card majors,
   and North plays an aggressive game.

♠: 8 6 4
♡: 9 6 3
◇: A K 6 3
♣: K 9 5

♠: A K 10
♡: A J 10 8 4 2
◇: 5 2
♣: 7 3

The play:
1 West leads ♠3: four, nine, **ten**
2 **South plays** ♡**A:** *West discards* ♣*6.*

Plan South's play.

40

Teams, dealer North,
neither side vulnerable.

The bidding:

WEST	NORTH	EAST	SOUTH
	2 ♣*	Pass	2 NT**
Pass	3 ◇***	Pass	3 NT
Pass	Pass	Pass	

   * 4-4-4-1 shape, 12-15 points
  ** Where is your singleton?
*** In diamonds

West holds:

♠: K Q J 6 4 3
♡: 10 9 2
◇: 3
♣: 7 3 2

What should West lead?

37. Majoring in card reading

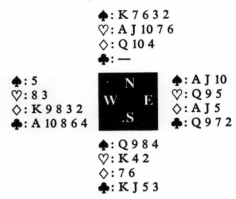

♠: K 7 6 3 2
♡: A J 10 7 6
◇: Q 10 4
♣: —

♠: 5
♡: 8 3
◇: K 9 8 3 2
♣: A 10 8 6 4

♠: A J 10
♡: Q 9 5
◇: A J 5
♣: Q 9 7 2

♠: Q 9 8 4
♡: K 4 2
◇: 7 6
♣: K J 5 3

South was lucky to escape an initial diamond lead, and he has already negotiated one hurdle successfully by playing a low spade (rather than the king of spades, hoping to pin an honour in the West hand) from dummy at trick two.

When the queen of spades wins the second trick, South has to make a decision about how the trumps are breaking. Both the bidding and the play make it appear likely that the trumps will be 3–1 rather than 2–2. In that case South cannot afford to play a second trump before he has set up the hearts for a diamond discard.

The key to the right play in hearts is again to be found in the bidding (East's 1 NT bid). South should lead a low heart to the ace and run the jack of hearts on the way back. A third heart to the king is followed by a club ruff, and the lead of an established heart winner from dummy allows South to discard a losing diamond as East trumps with a natural trump winner.

38. Easy does it

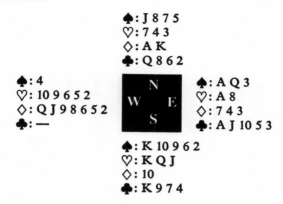

♠: J 8 7 5
♡: 7 4 3
◇: A K
♣: Q 8 6 2

♠: 4
♡: 10 9 6 5 2
◇: Q J 9 8 6 5 2
♣: —

♠: A Q 3
♡: A 8
◇: 7 4 3
♣: A J 10 5 3

♠: K 10 9 6 2
♡: K Q J
◇: 10
♣: K 9 7 4

In practice East botched the defence. He rose with the ace of spades and played the ace and another club, aiming to give West a club ruff. But West was out of trumps, and the declarer had no trouble in making ten tricks.

After the hand, East rebuked his partner for seeking a club ruff (via the suit-preference lead of the two of diamonds) when he had only a singleton trump. But, of course, the ◇2 lead could have been vital if East had held the diamond ace.

East was guilty of failing to make use of the available information. Since North-South were playing five-card majors, West could have no more than one trump. But if West could be placed with a void in clubs, it was obvious that South must have four clubs. All East had to do was to win the ace of spades, cash the ace of hearts, and sit back and wait for two club tricks.

It is one thing to work out what partner's lead means; it is another to apply the knowledge correctly.

39. Good news, bad news

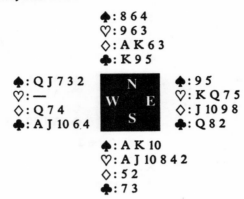

♠: 8 6 4
♡: 9 6 3
◇: A K 6 3
♣: K 9 5

♠: Q J 7 3 2
♡: —
◇: Q 7 4
♣: A J 10 6 4

♠: 9 5
♡: K Q 7 5
◇: J 10 9 8
♣: Q 8 2

♠: A K 10
♡: A J 10 8 4 2
◇: 5 2
♣: 7 3

The opening lead was a stroke of luck for the declarer, but it will do South no good to complain about his partner's overbidding and the unlucky trump split if North is able to retort that he should have made the contract.

At the table the declarer failed when he played a trump to dummy's nine at trick three. East won the queen and returned his last spade. On winning the next trump, East led a club to his partner's ace and ruffed the spade return to put the contract one down.

After the bad news at trick two, South knows that the contract cannot succeed unless the ace of clubs is with West. He also knows that West almost certainly has five spades for his overcall. Hence South should foresee what will happen on a trump continuation.

The correct play is to lead a club at trick three. If West goes in with the ace, South can revert to playing trumps when he regains the lead. If West ducks and the king of clubs wins, South must continue with a second club in order to cut communications between East and West. The trumps can wait.

40. Out of sequence

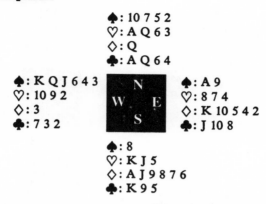

♠: 10 7 5 2
♡: A Q 6 3
♢: Q
♣: A Q 6 4

♠: K Q J 6 4 3
♡: 10 9 2
♢: 3
♣: 7 3 2

♠: A 9
♡: 8 7 4
♢: K 10 5 4 2
♣: J 10 8

♠: 8
♡: K J 5
♢: A J 9 8 7 6
♣: K 9 5

In an international match West led the ten of hearts and the declarer eventually made ten tricks.

A case can be made for a heart lead. A diamond is certainly not indicated (East would have doubled 3 ♢ with very strong diamonds), and a major suit lead is better than a lead from those anaemic clubs.

Take half marks for a heart lead, and half marks for leading a spade honour (which could work if South is void, but blocks the suit here). To earn full marks you have to lead a *low* spade. When you have three honours in sequence and dummy or declarer is known to have at least a four-card holding in the suit, lead fourth-highest rather than top of the sequence against no trumps.

The lead of a low card may yield a different benefit. In the 1971 Bermuda Bowl, Deal 2 of Round Ten had this club distribution:

A 10 8 5
K Q J 7 2   9 6
4 3

Against 3 NT, Tim Seres found the devastating ♣2 lead through dummy's first bid suit. Declarer naturally finessed the eight and the nine won. Clubs were continued, and since West had a side entry the defenders made five tricks. No other defence would have prevailed.

41

Dealer South,
North-South vulnerable.

The bidding:

SOUTH	WEST	NORTH	EAST
1 NT	Pass	3 NT	End

♠: A Q
♡: 9 6 2
◇: J 6 4
♣: Q J 10 6 5

♠: K 4 3
♡: A K 5
◇: A 7 3
♣: K 4 3 2

West leads ◇5. Plan South's play.
(If you play low in dummy, East produces the ten; if you play dummy's jack, it is covered by East.)

42

Pairs, dealer South,
East-West vulnerable.

The bidding:

SOUTH	WEST	NORTH	EAST
1 NT*	Pass	Pass	Pass

* 12–14 points

♠: J 10 5 3
♡: 8 6 5 2
◇: 5
♣: A 10 4 3

♠: Q 9 7 4
♡: K Q 9
◇: K J 8 7
♣: K 6

The play:
1 West leads ♣5: three, **king,** eight
2 East leads ◇7: **queen,** ten, five
3 **South leads ♠A:** eight, three, seven
4 **South leads ♠K:** *West discards ♣2*
5 South leads ♠6: *West discards ◇3,* ♠J from dummy . . . .

How should East defend?

43

Teams, dealer North,
neither side vulnerable.

The bidding:

SOUTH	WEST	NORTH	EAST
		1 ♣	Double
2 ♠	3 ♡	3 ♠	4 ♡
4 ♠	Pass	Pass	Double
Pass	Pass	Pass	

♠: 9 3
♡: A 2
◇: J 9 3
♣: A K 10 7 6 3

♠: Q J 10 6 4 2
♡: 8 7
◇: A
♣: Q 9 4 2

West leads ♡Q. Plan South's play.

44

Dealer South,
both sides vulnerable.

The bidding:

SOUTH	WEST	NORTH	EAST
1 ♣	Pass	1 ♡	Pass
1 NT*	Pass	2 ♣	Pass
3 ♣	Pass	3 NT	End

* 12–14 points

♠: 10 7
♡: A 10 7 5
◇: A 9 5
♣: Q 7 6 2

♠: K Q 5
♡: 8 4
◇: J 10 6 3 2
♣: A 8 4

The play:
1 West leads ♠4: seven, **queen**, three
2 **East plays ♠K:** six from South, two from West.

Plan East's defence.

41. On the block where you live

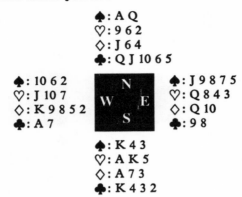

```
              ♠: A Q
              ♡: 9 6 2
              ◇: J 6 4
              ♣: Q J 10 6 5
♠: 10 6 2            ♠: J 9 8 7 5
♡: J 10 7           ♡: Q 8 4 3
◇: K 9 8 5 2        ◇: Q 10
♣: A 7             ♣: 9 8
              ♠: K 4 3
              ♡: A K 5
              ◇: A 7 3
              ♣: K 4 3 2
```

It is tempting to play the jack of diamonds from dummy at trick one and that is what the declarer did in practice. East covered with the queen and South ducked. When East continued with the ◇10 South again played low, but West overtook with the king and cleared the diamond suit. West regained the lead with the ace of clubs and cashed out for one down.

Declarer does not need two diamond tricks for his contract and he should do his best to protect himself against the diamond attack. There is no problem if the diamonds are 4–3, of course. If they are 5–2, playing the jack works when West has led from K Q x x x, while playing low from dummy, winning the ace works when West has led from K x x x x or Q x x x x. Then East has Q x or K x and the play of the ace at trick one blocks the suit. The latter situation is the more likely, so it is correct to play low from dummy and win the ace of diamonds at trick one.

42. Making matchpoints from mangling

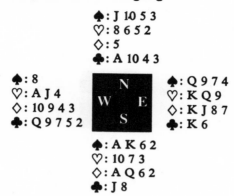

♠: J 10 5 3
♡: 8 6 5 2
◇: 5
♣: A 10 4 3

♠: 8
♡: A J 4
◇: 10 9 4 3
♣: Q 9 7 5 2

♠: Q 9 7 4
♡: K Q 9
◇: K J 8 7
♣: K 6

♠: A K 6 2
♡: 10 7 3
◇: A Q 6 2
♣: J 8

South has already shown up with thirteen points (♠: A K, ◇: A Q) and cannot have more than a jack extra. West's ♣2 indicates that he started with five clubs, which means that the declarer has no chance of making his contract unless he began with J x in clubs.

If East wins ♠Q and returns a diamond, South wins, runs ♣J, and crosses to the ten of spades to cash ♣A. East can prevent this either by ducking ♠J or by winning and returning his last spade to eliminate the entry to dummy. When East later regains the lead it would be wise for him to return his club, thus making it easy for West to duck declarer's jack.

The declarer mangled the hand, of course. He could have unblocked ♣J at trick one to make sure of two club tricks. Alternatively, after cashing the top spades, he could have led ♣J before the third round of spades. It would not be polite to mention these points or to extol the. virtues of Stayman.

43. Severance pays

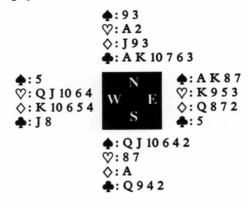

♠: 9 3
♡: A 2
◇: J 9 3
♣: A K 10 7 6 3

♠: 5
♡: Q J 10 6 4
◇: K 10 6 5 4
♣: J 8

♠: A K 8 7
♡: K 9 5 3
◇: Q 8 7 2
♣: 5

♠: Q J 10 6 4 2
♡: 8 7
◇: A
♣: Q 9 4 2

The average player takes the ace of hearts and immediately tackles trumps. The expert play, however, is to duck the first heart. On the actual lie of the cards this is a very necessary safeguard.

At one table in a teams match the declarer won ♡A and played a spade. East won with the king and switched to his singleton club. On regaining the lead with ♠A, East put his partner in with a heart and received a club ruff to put the contract one down.

At the other table the declarer ducked the heart lead, making this defence impossible as there was no longer any entry to the West hand.

It could cost to duck the first heart if West had two small trumps and a singleton club and switched to the club at trick two. In view of East's two doubles, however, it is much more likely that he has the singleton club along with four trumps.

44. What's the hurry ?

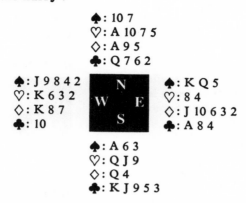

```
                    ♠: 10 7
                    ♡: A 10 7 5
                    ◇: A 9 5
                    ♣: Q 7 6 2
  ♠: J 9 8 4 2          N          ♠: K Q 5
  ♡: K 6 3 2      W          E      ♡: 8 4
  ◇: K 8 7                          ◇: J 10 6 3 2
  ♣: 10                 S          ♣: A 8 4
                    ♠: A 6 3
                    ♡: Q J 9
                    ◇: Q 4
                    ♣: K J 9 5 3
```

East's problem is whether to continue spades, playing West for A 9 8 4 2, or switch to diamonds.

A little thought indicates that East should switch to the three of diamonds. If West did begin with five spades headed by the ace, declarer can at best make seven tricks in the red suits before letting East in with the ace of clubs. Therefore East has time for two bites at the cherry.

At the table, East hastily played a third spade. Declarer won, knocked out the ace of clubs, and took the heart finesse for ten tricks.

The presence of the nine of diamonds in dummy precludes a lead of the jack at trick three. On the lead of a low diamond declarer will, in practice rise with the queen unless he is a beginner or has seen your cards (in the former case you have a sufficient edge, in the latter you know what to do).

Three down should induce in North-South a healthy respect for your defence, and they should be less eager to bid game on flimsy values in future.

45

♠: 9 7 6 4 2
♡: K Q 5
◇: 4
♣: A Q 10 3

South plays in six diamonds after an
auction that will not be found in 'Great
Bidding Sequences of the Seventies'.

♠: A J 3
♡: A
◇: A 9 8 7 6 5 3 2
♣: J

How should South plan the play:
a) on a heart lead ?
b) on a spade lead ?
c) on the lead of the ♣4 ?

46

Pairs, dealer South,
East-West vulnerable.

The bidding:

SOUTH	WEST	NORTH	EAST
1 ◇	Pass	1 ♠	Pass
2 NT*	Pass	Pass	Pass

* 17–18 points

♠: K 6 4 2
♡: 8 2
◇: Q 4 3
♣: J 9 6 2

♠: A Q 10 9 5
♡: 10 3
◇: A 7 2
♣: 8 4 3

The play:
1 West leads ♡5: two, ten, **king**
2 South leads ◇6 to dummy's queen, West playing the eight . . . .
Plan East's defence.
(If East ducks, diamonds are continued.)

47

Teams, dealer South,
North-South vulnerable.

The bidding:

SOUTH	WEST	NORTH	EAST
2 NT	Pass	3 ♣	Pass
3 NT	Pass	Pass	Pass

♠: Q 9 7 6
♡: J 8 7 5
◇: J 10
♣: Q 6 5

♠: A K 4
♡: A 9
◇: K 9 3
♣: A K 9 4 3

The play:
1 West leads ◇6: **jack,** five, nine.

How should South continue?

48

Dealer North,
East-West vulnerable.

The bidding:

WEST	NORTH	EAST	SOUTH
	1 ♣	Pass	1 ♠
Pass	2 ♠	Pass	4 ♠
Pass	Pass	Pass	

♠: A 7 4 3
♡: J 10 3
◇: Q 6
♣: A Q 10 6

♠: 10 2
♡: A 7
◇: A 8 5 4
♣: 9 8 7 5 4

West leads ♡K. Plan East's defence.

45. Making the most of Lady Luck

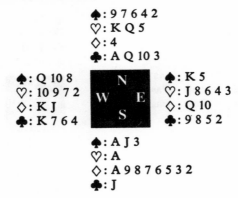

♠: 9 7 6 4 2
♡: K Q 5
◇: 4
♣: A Q 10 3

♠: Q 10 8
♡: 10 9 7 2
◇: K J
♣: K 7 6 4

N
W E
S

♠: K 5
♡: J 8 6 4 3
◇: Q 10
♣: 9 8 5 2

♠: A J 3
♡: A
◇: A 9 8 7 6 5 3 2
♣: J

If the slam is to succeed, you will need to be lucky enough to find the trumps divided 2–2.

a) On a heart lead win ♡A, cross your fingers, and play ace and another diamond. Later you can cross to ♣A and discard your two losing spades on the hearts.

b) On a spade lead win ♠A, cash ♡A, play ♣J to dummy's ace and take your discards on the king and queen of hearts at once. Then play the ace and another diamond.

c) On a club lead you need a further slice of luck, for you have to risk the finesse. Play the queen from dummy at trick one, continue with the ace of clubs and discard your ace of hearts. Having removed that blockage, you can discard the losing spades on the king and queen of hearts. The ace and another diamond will then see you to success and more overbidding in the future.

46. Wait for the signal

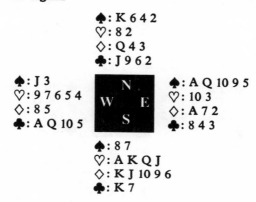

♠: K 6 4 2
♡: 8 2
◇: Q 4 3
♣: J 9 6 2

♠: J 3
♡: 9 7 6 5 4
◇: 8 5
♣: A Q 10 5

♠: A Q 10 9 5
♡: 10 3
◇: A 7 2
♣: 8 4 3

♠: 8 7
♡: A K Q J
◇: K J 10 9 6
♣: K 7

East should hold up his ace of diamonds until the third round. There can be no urgency to return a heart, because if West has the top hearts South cannot come to eight tricks without the diamond suit (at most he can make four clubs, two diamonds and a heart). In any case it is unlikely that the defence can run the hearts. West would not have led the ♡5 from A Q J x x or Q J 9 x x (the normal lead would be the queen).

Holding up the ace of diamonds allows West to signal how the defence should continue. On the third diamond West will discard the ♣10 or the ♡4, either of which gives the right message. East can then switch to ♣8, leading a high pip to deny interest in the suit. West will win and return the jack of spades, and the defence must come to three spades (five if declarer goes up with dummy's king), two clubs and a diamond.

South's 2 NT rebid is somewhat off-beat, but the no trump syndrome in the pairs game is as incurable as the common cold. Note that if East wins the ace of diamonds and returns a heart, declarer wraps up eight tricks.

47. Safe and sound

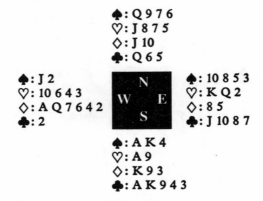

♠: Q 9 7 6
♡: J 8 7 5
◇: J 10
♣: Q 6 5

♠: J 2
♡: 10 6 4 3
◇: A Q 7 6 4 2
♣: 2

♠: 10 8 5 3
♡: K Q 2
◇: 8 5
♣: J 10 8 7

♠: A K 4
♡: A 9
◇: K 9 3
♣: A K 9 4 3

The straightforward method of playing the hand is to cash the queen of clubs and continue with a club to the ace or king. If the suit breaks 3–2 there is no problem. If West proves to have four clubs, you can safely concede a club trick and establish the suit. If East has four clubs, you can always fall back on the spades. This method of play will succeed nine times out of ten.

Once East follows to the first club, however, you can make certain of nine tricks by inserting your nine of clubs if East plays low on the second round. If East plays an honour and West shows out, return to dummy with the third round of spades and take the marked club finesse.

On the actual hand it would work equally well to finesse the ♣9 on the first round, but playing the queen first has the advantage of picking up all the tricks when West has ♣J or ♣10 singleton and when East has 10 x or J x in clubs.

48. Observe the Golden Rule

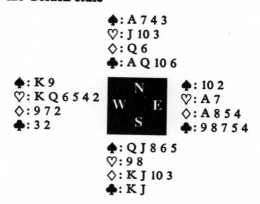

♠: A 7 4 3
♥: J 10 3
♦: Q 6
♣: A Q 10 6

♠: K 9
♥: K Q 6 5 4 2
♦: 9 7 2
♣: 3 2

♠: 10 2
♥: A 7
♦: A 8 5 4
♣: 9 8 7 5 4

♠: Q J 8 6 5
♥: 9 8
♦: K J 10 3
♣: K J

The defence will vary according to the standard of the player.
The novice will play the seven of hearts and block the suit. He will still defeat the contract if West holds the king of diamonds, but on the actual hand he lets the declarer home.

The average player, recognizing that the lead is from K Q, overtakes the king with the ace and returns the seven of hearts. This works on the actual hand. West wins and plays a third heart, and East's uppercut with the ♣10 produces a trump trick for West. But suppose South began with ♠: K Q J 9 8 6, ♥: 9 8, ♦: J 10 9, ♣: K J. It will not be easy for West, after winning the second heart, to find the diamond switch away from his king. And if he leads anything else declarer will run ten straight tricks.

The expert covers every contingency. He overtakes the king of hearts with his ace, cashes the ace of diamonds, and then reverts to hearts. No matter what the position, West should then be able to find the correct continuation. Expert defence aims to clarify the position for partner whenever possible.

Golden Rule of Defence: Don't give partner a chance to go wrong.

Part three Advanced level

The problems in this final section are assessed as fairly difficult. The average player will be doing well to score better than 50%. To obtain maximum benefit, you should make a genuine effort to solve the problems. Although they are not simple, each question admits of a logical answer and the necessary clues are to be found in the bidding and early play.

49

North opens a weak no trump
and, regrettably, the
partnership reaches:

♠: 10 6 5
♡: Q 7
◇: K Q 7 4
♣: A J 3 2

a) Four spades,
b) Five spades.

♠: A 8 7 4 3
♡: K 8
◇: A J 6
♣: K Q 9

In each case West leads the three of hearts to his partner's ace and East
returns a heart.
Plan the play for both contracts.

50

♠: A J 10 9 7
♡: 7 6 5 4 3
◇: A 10
♣: J

♠: Q 4 3 2
♡: K J 10 9
◇: K 7 6 2
♣: 4

Teams, dealer North,
East-West vulnerable.

The bidding:

WEST	NORTH	EAST	SOUTH
	Pass	Pass	3 NT*
Pass	Pass	Pass	

* Solid minor suit with perhaps
a little outside strength

The play:
1 West leads ♡J: **East wins the ace,** South drops the queen
2 East returns ♡8: *South discards ◇8*
3 **West cashes** ♡10: *South discards ◇9*
4 **West cashes** ♡K: *East discards ♣5, South discards ◇5.*

How should West continue?

51

Teams, dealer North,
both sides vulnerable.

♠: Q 6 5 4
♡: A K Q 7
◇: 9 8 5
♣: 6 2

The bidding:

WEST	NORTH	EAST	SOUTH
	Pass	Pass	1 ♡
Pass	3 ♡	Pass	5 ♡
Pass	6 ♡	End	

♠: —
♡: 10 9 6 4 3
◇: A K J 4
♣: A K J 9

The play:
1 West leads ♡2: **ace**, eight, three
2 ♡**K is played from dummy**: jack, four, five.

How should declarer play?
What would your answer be at match-pointed pairs (a) in a weak field?
(b) in a strong field?

52

Teams, dealer North,
North-South vulnerable.
The bidding:

WEST	NORTH	EAST	SOUTH
	2 ♣*	4 ♡	4 ♠
Pass	Pass	5 ♣	Double
5 ♡	5 ♠	End	

* Precision System, shows five or more clubs and 11–15 points

You, West, hold:

♠: 10 9 6 4
♡: 10 2
◇: 8 6 4
♣: A J 6 5

Assuming partner's sanity, what lead do you make?

49. It costs nothing to try

♠: 10 6 5
♡: Q 7
◇: K Q 7 4
♣: A J 3 2

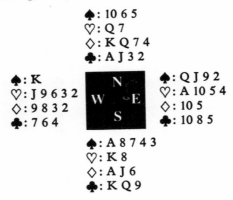

♠: K
♡: J 9 6 3 2
◇: 9 8 3 2
♣: 7 6 4

♠: Q J 9 2
♡: A 10 5 4
◇: 10 5
♣: 10 8 5

♠: A 8 7 4 3
♡: K 8
◇: A J 6
♣: K Q 9

a) In four spades your only concern is to avoid losing three trump tricks. There will be no problem if trumps are 3–2, but that does not mean you should simply bang out ace and another trump and hope for the best. You can give yourself a slight extra chance by crossing to dummy and leading the ten of trumps. This cannot cost in any layout and is the genuine way to hold your trump losers to two if East began with K Q 2 and West with the singleton nine. But leading the ten also gives you a psychological chance, for East may cover from K Q 9 2, K J 9 2 or Q J 9 2.

At the table East did cover the ten, thereby telescoping three trump tricks into two. If East had given it any thought he would have realized that there was nothing to gain by covering, but the habits of a lifetime are not easily broken.

b) In five spades there is no genuine play for the contract, but the best shot is to lead a low trump towards the ten. You hope that West will go up from J 9 2 or Q 9 2, thus colliding with his partner's doubleton honours and limiting your trump losers to one. This is not much of a hope and it won't work against competent opposition, but who plays against competent opposition all the time?

50. One small hope

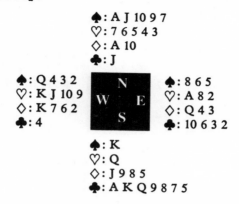

♠ : A J 10 9 7
♡ : 7 6 5 4 3
◇ : A 10
♣ : J

♠ : Q 4 3 2
♡ : K J 10 9
◇ : K 7 6 2
♣ : 4

♠ : 8 6 5
♡ : A 8 2
◇ : Q 4 3
♣ : 10 6 3 2

♠ : K
♡ : Q
◇ : J 9 8 5
♣ : A K Q 9 8 7 5

South is marked with a long and solid club suit, but some solid suits are solider than others. Clearly there is no hope for the defence if South's clubs are as good as A K Q 10 x x x. West must defend on the assumption that his partner has four clubs headed by the ten.

Even then, South may still be able to make his contract if he has some means of reaching his hand after cashing the club jack in dummy. Holding the king of diamonds himself, West can see that the only card of entry the declarer can hold is the king of spades. Indeed South is likely to hold the king in view of East's discard of ♠5 at trick four.

West should therefore switch to a spade, hoping the king is singleton, in an attempt to knock out South's entry before the clubs can be unblocked. This is the only defence that offers any hope of defeating the contract.

51. Safest needle in the haystack

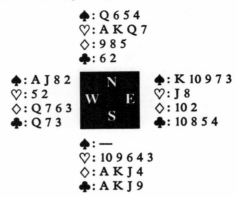

♠: Q 6 5 4
♡: A K Q 7
◇: 9 8 5
♣: 6 2

♠: A J 8 2
♡: 5 2
◇: Q 7 6 3
♣: Q 7 3

♠: K 10 9 7 3
♡: J 8
◇: 10 2
♣: 10 8 5 4

♠: —
♡: 10 9 6 4 3
◇: A K J 4
♣: A K J 9

At the table the declarer finessed the ♣J at trick three. West won and tried to cash ♠A. South ruffed, played ♣A and ♣K pitching a diamond, then ◇A, ◇K, diamond ruffed. As neither the queen of diamonds nor the ten of clubs had appeared, declarer had to go down.

The declarer was unlucky, to be sure, but he did not avail himself of the chance of a doubleton ◇10. There are many possible lines of play and the following offers the best chance of success. First play off the ace and king of diamonds. If either ◇Q or ◇10 drops, you are home. If a diamond honour does not appear, continue with the ace and king of clubs and ruff ♣9 in dummy. Then lead a diamond from the table towards your J x. This line is bound to succeed unless West has four or more diamonds headed by the queen and ten, and it succeeds even then if ♣Q drops in three rounds.

At pairs, in a weak field, not many will reach the slam and you should still adopt the safest line. In a good field most pairs will bid the slam and you must try for an overtrick. The best shot is to take the diamond finesse. If it fails, cash a top diamond to see if ◇10 appears. If it doesn't cash another top diamond and, if the suit does not break 3–3, ruff the fourth diamond and take the club finesse.

52. Applying information received

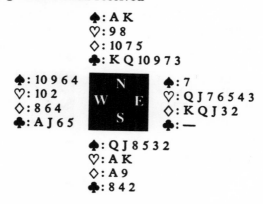

♠: A K
♡: 9 8
◇: 10 7 5
♣: K Q 10 9 7 3

♠: 10 9 6 4
♡: 10 2
◇: 8 6 4
♣: A J 6 5

N
W E
S

♠: 7
♡: Q J 7 6 5 4 3
◇: K Q J 3 2
♣: —

♠: Q J 8 5 3 2
♡: A K
◇: A 9
♣: 8 4 2

East was prepared to sacrifice at the five-level, and his bid of five clubs was intended to indicate a lead against five spades if the opponents pushed on. Since West is looking at the ace of clubs, it should be clear to him that his partner's lead-directing bid must be based on a void.

At the table, having deduced all this, West led the ace and another club. East ruffed the second club, but that was the end of the road for the defence. The declarer won the diamond switch, played off the ace and king of spades, returned with a heart to draw the remaining trumps, and eventually discarded his diamond loser on dummy's clubs.

This turn of events was foreseeable, and West should have retained control of the club suit by leading a low club at trick one. East ruffs and switches to the king of diamonds, and the defenders are bound to come to three tricks.

53

Pairs, dealer North,
both sides vulnerable.

The bidding:

WEST	NORTH	EAST	SOUTH
	1 ♣	Pass	1 NT*
2 ♡	2 NT**	Pass	3 NT
Pass	Pass	Pass	

* Artificial, game force
** 12–14 flat, with heart stopper

♠: A J 3
♡: A 10 3
◇: 10 9 6
♣: Q J 8 7

♠: K Q 6
♡: 9
◇: K J 4 3
♣: A 10 9 5 3

The pairs game is not conducive to bidding elegance, but your job is to bring in three no trumps.
West leads the king of hearts. Plan South's play.
(If you duck the first heart, East plays the seven and West continues with ♡6).

54

♠: 6
♡: A K 9 5
◇: Q J 3
♣: A K Q 8 2

♠: K Q 9 5 3
♡: 8 6 4 3 2
◇: K 8 5
♣: —

Teams, dealer North,
East-West vulnerable.

The bidding:

WEST	NORTH	EAST	SOUTH
	1 ♣*	Pass	3 NT**
Pass	4 ♣***	Pass	4 ♡
Pass	6 ♡	End	

* Precision, 16 or more points, any shape
** 12–13 points, 4-3-3-3 distribution
*** Asking for four-card suit

The play:
1 West leads ♠K: six, two, **ace**
2 South leads ♠7: three, *ruffed with ♡A*, four
3 The ♣2 is led from dummy: three, jack . . . .

How should West plan the defence?

55

Rubber, dealer North,
North-South vulnerable.

The bidding:

WEST	NORTH	EAST	SOUTH
	1 ♣	Pass	1 ♠
Pass	2 ♡	Pass	2 NT
Pass	3 ♠	Pass	4 ♠
Double	Pass	Pass	Pass

♠: A K 9
♡: A 7 4 3
♢: 6
♣: K Q 8 6 2

♠: J 7 6 3 2
♡: K 8 6
♢: A 8 7 2
♣: 4

The play:
1 West leads ♠4: **ace wins,** *East discards* ♢5
2 ♡3 is led from dummy: queen, **king,** nine
3 South leads ♣4: five, **king,** three.

How should South continue?

56

♠: Q J 8 6 3
♡: A K J 6 3
♢: 5 3
♣: 5

♠: A 10 9 7
♡: 7 2
♢: A 6
♣: A 9 8 7 4

Dealer South,
East-West vulnerable.

The bidding:

SOUTH	WEST	NORTH	EAST
1 ♠	Pass	4 ♠	End

The play:
1 **West leads ♣A:** five, two, ten
2 **West leads ♢A:** three, two, seven.

How should West continue?

53. From the right side

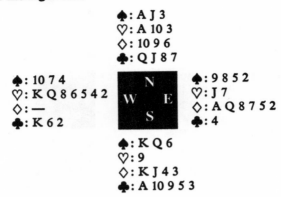

♠: A J 3
♡: A 10 3
◇: 10 9 6
♣: Q J 8 7

♠: 10 7 4   ♠: 9 8 5 2
♡: K Q 8 6 5 4 2   ♡: J 7
◇: —   ◇: A Q 8 7 5 2
♣: K 6 2   ♣: 4

♠: K Q 6
♡: 9
◇: K J 4 3
♣: A 10 9 5 3

At the table the declarer won the second round of hearts. This was not an outstanding success, for when the club finesse lost West cashed the rest of the hearts for down three. Similar results ensued where North was declarer and East began with ♡J. At one table South made overtricks on the lead of the ♡6. He played low in dummy, East reasonably played the seven, and the ♡9 made a surprise trick.

Where the ♡K is led, South succeeds by winning the first round or holding up twice. If ♡A is played at trick one, the club finesse loses but the hearts are blocked.

If declarer ducks the first heart, he must also duck the second. When East wins he is unable to continue the attack. But ducking twice could prove expensive if West held the queen of diamonds as well as the king of clubs. After the second heart East could switch to a diamond, and the defence could take two hearts, two diamonds and a club.

The correct play is to win the ♡A at trick one, hoping for either the club finesse to work or for East to have ♡J doubleton.

54. When the time is ripe

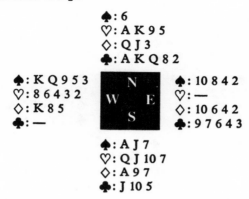

♠: 6
♡: A K 9 5
◇: Q J 3
♣: A K Q 8 2

♠: K Q 9 5 3   ♠: 10 8 4 2
♡: 8 6 4 3 2   ♡: —
◇: K 8 5   ◇: 10 6 4 2
♣: —   ♣: 9 7 6 4 3

♠: A J 7
♡: Q J 10 7
◇: A 9 7
♣: J 10 5

This hand should be easy to defend because the South hand is an open book. The declarer is known to have started with a 3–4–3–3 shape, and he must have every missing high card except perhaps for the jack of spades.

If East had the ten of clubs, it would be a sufficient defence for West to ruff the ♣J and exit with ♠Q or a trump. But on the actual hand this allows declarer to make in comfort. He wins a heart return in hand, ruffs ♠J high, draws trumps and claims.

There is no need for West to bank on his partner having a club stopper. He can make certain of defeating the contract by refusing to ruff clubs until the third round, thus cutting declarer off from dummy. After drawing trumps, South will have no way of returning to the table to cash the remaining clubs. In fact, since West has the king of diamonds, he can still defeat the contract if he waits until the fourth round of clubs before ruffing.

55. Wrong place at the right time

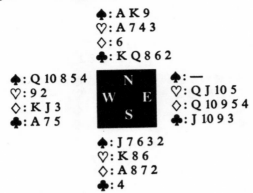

♠ : A K 9
♡ : A 7 4 3
◇ : 6
♣ : K Q 8 6 2

♠ : Q 10 8 5 4
♡ : 9 2
◇ : K J 3
♣ : A 7 5

N
W   E
S

♠ : —
♡ : Q J 10 5
◇ : Q 10 9 5 4
♣ : J 10 9 3

♠ : J 7 6 3 2
♡ : K 8 6
◇ : A 8 7 2
♣ : 4

At the table the declarer failed in the following manner. He ruffed a club at trick four, played a heart to the ace, and ruffed another club, dropping the ace. Then he cashed the ace of diamonds and ruffed a diamond, leaving the five-card position shown below.

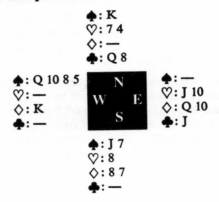

♠ : K
♡ : 7 4
◇ : —
♣ : Q 8

♠ : Q 10 8 5
♡ : —
◇ : K
♣ : —

N
W   E
S

♠ : —
♡ : J 10
◇ : Q 10
♣ : J

♠ : J 7
♡ : 8
◇ : 8 7
♣ : —

South continued with the ♣Q from dummy, throwing his heart loser. West ruffed and led a trump, and nothing could prevent West from making the last three tricks.

This was simply a case of mistiming. South needs to ruff not one but two diamonds in dummy. After a heart to the ace at trick five, he should continue with a diamond to the ace, a diamond ruff and a club ruff.

The five-card ending is the same, with the vital difference that the lead is in the South hand. South ruffs a diamond with ♠K and leads any card from dummy, playing his losing heart from hand. West, trump-bound, has to give declarer his tenth trick with the jack of spades.

56. Early recognition

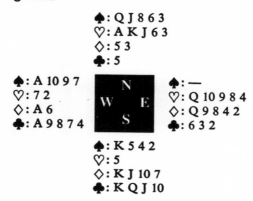

                ♠ : Q J 8 6 3
                ♡ : A K J 6 3
                ◇ : 5 3
                ♣ : 5

♠ : A 10 9 7   ♠ : —
♡ : 7 2   ♡ : Q 10 9 8 4
◇ : A 6   ◇ : Q 9 8 4 2
♣ : A 9 8 7 4   ♣ : 6 3 2

                ♠ : K 5 4 2
                ♡ : 5
                ◇ : K J 10 7
                ♣ : K Q J 10

In the 1970 Bermuda Bowl, West switched to hearts and the declarer made his contract. He won the ace of hearts, led the three of spades to the king and ace, won the diamond return and cashed two clubs, throwing hearts from dummy. A spade to the ten and jack was followed by a ruff of the heart jack and a further spade finesse.

West went astray through failure to recognize his problem in time. He should have realized that he had the contract beaten if he could prevent South from entering his hand twice *after* he found out about the 4–0 trump split. The only entry in the South hand that is vulnerable to immediate attack is in diamonds, and West should therefore lead a second diamond at trick three.

South wins and plays ♠K. West takes his ace and exits with a heart. Now South can return to hand by ruffing the second heart and cash a couple of clubs, as before, but when he leads a spade West puts in the nine or ten. Stuck in dummy, South has to concede a second trump trick to West.

57

Rubber, dealer West,
East-West vulnerable.

The bidding:

WEST	NORTH	EAST	SOUTH
Pass	Pass	Pass	2 NT
Pass	3 NT	End	

♠: 10 7 5 4
♡: K 9 8
◇: 10 3 2
♣: K J 9

♠: A K J
♡: J 4
◇: A K J 5
♣: A 10 4 2

Against expert defenders,
the play goes:
1 West leads ♡2: eight, **queen,** four
2 East returns ♡6: jack, **ace,** nine
3 West plays ♡5: **king,** three . . . .

What should South discard, and how should he plan the play?

58

♠: 2
♡: 10 8 4
◇: A 10 3 2
♣: Q J 9 6 2

♠: 10 9 8 3
♡: A K Q 7 2
◇: J 6
♣: 8 4

Teams, dealer North,
North-South vulnerable.

The bidding:

WEST	NORTH	EAST	SOUTH
	Pass	4 ◇	4 ♠
Pass	Pass	Pass	

The play:
1 **West leads ♡K:** four, six, five
2 **West leads ♡Q:** eight, three, nine
3 **West leads ♡A:** *East discards the ◇9.*

How should West continue?

59

Teams, dealer South,
North-South vulnerable.

♠: J 10 2
♡: K 9 8
◇: 8 6 3
♣: 9 7 6 2

The bidding:

SOUTH	WEST	NORTH	EAST
1 ♠	2 ♡	Pass	4 ♡
4 ♠	Pass	Pass	Double
Pass	Pass	Pass	

♠: A K 9 8 6 4
♡: 6
◇: A Q J 7 2
♣: 4

The play:
1 **West leads ♣K:** two, five, four
2 **West switches to ♡Q:** eight, seven, six
3 ...... leads ♡J: nine, three, *ruffed with ♠4.*

How should South continue?

60

Rubber, dealer South,
neither side vulnerable.

♠: A 9 3
♡: A K 7 6 5 4
◇: 9 8 3
♣: 6

The bidding:

SOUTH	WEST	NORTH	EAST
3 ◇	5 ♣	5 ◇	End

♠: J 10 7 6
♡: Q J 10 9 8
◇: 10
♣: A 7 3

The play:
1 West leads ♡3: **ace**, eight, two
2 ◇3 is led from dummy: ten, queen, **ace**
3 West plays ♣10: six, **ace**, eight.

How should East continue?

57. Home is where the heart is

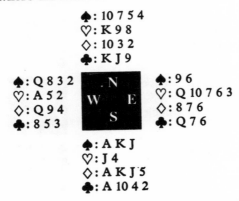

♠: 10 7 5 4
♡: K 9 8
◇: 10 3 2
♣: K J 9

♠: Q 8 3 2
♡: A 5 2
◇: Q 9 4
♣: 8 5 3

♠: 9 6
♡: Q 10 7 6 3
◇: 8 7 6
♣: Q 7 6

♠: A K J
♡: J 4
◇: A K J 5
♣: A 10 4 2

In practice the declarer failed when he placed the long hearts with West and took the club finesse into the 'safe' hand. East cashed two more hearts for one down.

East's play in hearts (Q, 6, 3) is not consistent with a four-card holding, but tallies with either a three-card or a five-card suit. The clue to the location of the hearts lies in the second trick. Had West, an expert defender, started with five hearts (and led ♡2 as a false card), he would not have won the second round of hearts but would have ducked to keep communication with East. As West does not have five hearts and East does not have four, the actual position can be pin-pointed.

South should discard the jack of spades on the third heart, cash the king of clubs and then run the nine. (a) If ♣9 loses to the queen, the ♣J provides an entry to take the diamond finesse into the safe hand. (b) If the ♣9 holds, South should switch to diamonds and finesse the jack. To repeat the club finesse could be expensive if West has held up the queen, for there would be no entry left in dummy for the diamond finesse.

58. Trusting partner

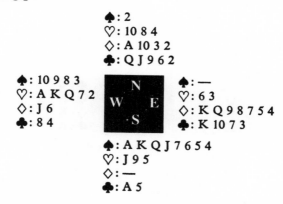

♠: 2
♡: 10 8 4
◇: A 10 3 2
♣: Q J 9 6 2

♠: 10 9 8 3
♡: A K Q 7 2
◇: J 6
♣: 8 4

♠: —
♡: 6 3
◇: K Q 9 8 7 5 4
♣: K 10 7 3

♠: A K Q J 7 6 5 4
♡: J 9 5
◇: —
♣: A 5

The only continuation to defeat the contract is a trump. How can West deduce that?

The solution calls for a high degree of partnership co-operation and trust. Missing the ace, jack and ten of diamonds, East must surely have a seven-card suit for his opening bid of four diamonds. In that case he must know that the defence can never come to a diamond trick, so why did he signal with the nine of diamonds?

At the time when he made his discard, of course, East did not know whether West began with four hearts or five. But if he could over-ruff dummy (in the situation where West began with ♡: A K Q x and South with ♡: J x x x) East would discourage diamonds.

It follows that East cannot over-ruff dummy, which means that he must be void in trumps. South is therefore marked with eight spades, three hearts and two clubs, and West knows that only a trump lead can strand him in his own hand.

59. Enter once, enter twice

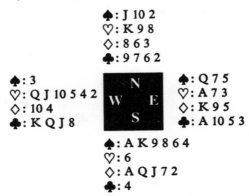

♠: J 10 2
♡: K 9 8
◇: 8 6 3
♣: 9 7 6 2

♠: 3
♡: Q J 10 5 4 2
◇: 10 4
♣: K Q J 8

♠: Q 7 5
♡: A 7 3
◇: K 9 5
♣: A 10 5 3

♠: A K 9 8 6 4
♡: 6
◇: A Q J 7 2
♣: 4

The winning play, not found at the table in an international tournament, is to lead the eight or nine of spades at trick four and play low in dummy East is faced with a dilemma. If the ♠Q is taken, there are two entries in dummy to take and repeat the diamond finesse. If the ♠Q is ducked, declarer draws trumps and concedes a trick to the king of diamonds.

The competing plays are inferior: (1) Ace and king of spades, hoping for the queen to drop. This is unlikely in view of East's double. (2) Low spade to the jack, or ace of spades and then a low spade to the jack. This gives only one entry to dummy and success will depend on the king of diamonds being doubleton with East.

If it turns out that East began with all four outstanding trumps, the recommended line is still the best. If East takes the queen of spades on the first round, you have your two entries. If East correctly ducks, you can continue with a low spade to the jack and hope that East has king doubleton in diamonds.

60. No hurry to help yourself

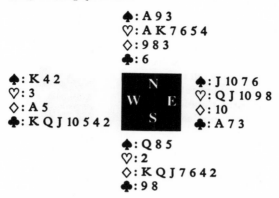

♠: A 9 3
♡: A K 7 6 5 4
◇: 9 8 3
♣: 6

♠: K 4 2
♡: 3
◇: A 5
♣: K Q J 10 5 4 2

♠: J 10 7 6
♡: Q J 10 9 8
◇: 10
♣: A 7 3

♠: Q 8 5
♡: 2
◇: K Q J 7 6 4 2
♣: 9 8

In practice East continued with a heart, hoping that South would discard or that West would be able to over-ruff. This turned out to be futile. South ruffed high, played a low trump to dummy (drawing West's last trump), ruffed another heart, ruffed a club and ruffed a third heart. A spade to dummy's ace then allowed South to discard his spade losers on the king of hearts and the established seven of hearts.

Had East returned a club or the jack of spades, the contract would have failed since dummy would have been short of an entry to set up the sixth heart. East could not blame his partner for leading the ten of clubs, as West was not to know that the declarer had also started with a singleton heart. In any case East could be almost certain that the ten of clubs was a false card.

East's defence would have worked if West's diamonds had been as good as doubleton ace and jack, but this possibility was a little remote compared with the probability of helping the declarer to set up the heart suit.

61

Teams,
neither side vulnerable.

North-South reach a contract of six
clubs. (As this book may fall into
innocent hands, the sequence is not
given. Assume that the situation was
desperate and that you needed to pick
up imps in a hurry)

♠: Q 10
♡: Q 6 5
♢: A J 10 5 4
♣: A Q 6

♠: A 3
♡: A 10 4 3
♢: 7 3
♣: K J 10 8 5

The play:
1 West leads ♣4: six, nine, **jack**
2 South leads ♢3: six, jack, **queen**
3 East returns ♠8 . . . .

Plan South's play to give him a chance of making the slam.

62

♠: A 10 8 5 4
♡: A Q 10
♢: 7 5
♣: 8 7 5

♠: 9 6
♡: K 9 8 3
♢: 10 9 4 3
♣: A J 4

Teams, dealer East,
North-South vulnerable.

The bidding:

WEST	NORTH	EAST	SOUTH
		Pass	2 ♣*
Pass	2 ♢**	Pass	2 NT***
Pass	3 ♠	Pass	3 NT
Pass	Pass	Pass	

   * Precision System, 11–15,
    at least five clubs
  ** Relay asking opener to
    describe hand
 *** Maximum opener, no
    second suit

The play:
1 West leads ♢3: five, **queen,** two
2 East returns ♢K: **ace,** four, seven
3 **South plays ♣K:** four, five, three
4 South plays ♠J: six, **ace,** three
5 ♣8 is led from dummy: *East discards ♡4,* ten, **jack.**

How should West continue ?

63

Teams, dealer West,
neither side vulnerable.

♠: Q 9
♡: J 8 6 3
◇: Q J 10
♣: K J 8 4

Both pairs are playing Acol,
using a 12–14 1 NT opening.

The bidding:

WEST	NORTH	EAST	SOUTH
1 ◇	Pass	2 ◇	4 ♠
Pass	Pass	Pass	

♠: K J 7 6 5 4 3
♡: A K Q 9
◇: 7
♣: 2

The play:
1 West leads ◇2: **East wins the ace**
2 East returns ♡2: **South wins the ace,** West plays the five.

Plan South's play.

64

Rubber,
North-South vulnerable.

♠: 4 2
♡: Q J 10 5 3
◇: 8 6
♣: A K 5 4

The bidding:

NORTH	SOUTH
1 ♡*	2 ◇
2 ♡	2 ♠
2 NT	5 ◇
Pass	

♠: A K
♡: A 7 6 4 2
◇: J 9 3
♣: 9 7 2

* Not given to underbidding

The play:
1 West leads ♣3: four, nine, **queen**
2 South leads ♠5: three, two, **king**
3 East leads ◇3: **ace,** four, six
4 South plays ♠6: seven, four, **ace.**

How should East continue?

61. Bid boldly, play desperately

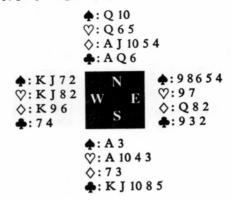

```
              ♠: Q 10
              ♡: Q 6 5
              ◇: A J 10 5 4
              ♣: A Q 6
♠: K J 7 2          N          ♠: 9 8 6 5 4
♡: K J 8 2     W       E       ♡: 9 7
◇: K 9 6                       ◇: Q 8 2
♣: 7 4              S          ♣: 9 3 2
              ♠: A 3
              ♡: A 10 4 3
              ◇: 7 3
              ♣: K J 10 8 5
```

It is, of course, correct to try to make the contract. On the assumption that a normal three no trumps is made in the other room, down one in six clubs costs 10 imps, down two 11 imps and down four 12 imps. Going more than one off is thus relatively inexpensive, while making six clubs will be a tremendous gain.

At trick three win the ace of spades (no sane East would return a spade from the king), play five rounds of trumps, throwing two hearts from dummy, then take the diamond finesse and run diamonds.

With the layout above, West is squeezed in a two-card ending. Dummy has ♠Q and ♡Q, South has ♡A and ♡10, and West has to unguard one of the major suits. For the squeeze to operate it is essential for South to cash all the clubs before the diamonds.

If you make six clubs in this manner and thereby win the match, don't expect to be on speaking terms with the opponents for a number of years (especially if you point out that West could have defeated you by playing ◇K at trick two, East by returning a diamond at trick three).

62. Cut him off

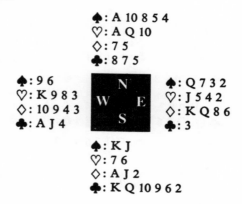

♠: A 10 8 5 4
♡: A Q 10
◇: 7 5
♣: 8 7 5

♠: 9 6
♡: K 9 8 3
◇: 10 9 4 3
♣: A J 4

♠: Q 7 3 2
♡: J 5 4 2
◇: K Q 8 6
♣: 3

♠: K J
♡: 7 6
◇: A J 2
♣: K Q 10 9 6 2

West should return the nine of spades, taking out South's entry to the clubs before the suit can be established.

South is known to have started with the king and queen of clubs, the ace and jack of diamonds (East played ◇Q at trick one) and the jack of spades. For his maximum opener he must hold ♠K as well, but he will not have a third spade since he did not support the suit.

Note that South makes his contract in comfort if West returns a diamond or a heart. On a spade return, South can do no better than take the heart finesse and set up the spades, making four spades, two hearts, one diamond and one club. East naturally has to co-operate by withholding ♠Q on the second round, and by returning ♡J or his fourth spade when in with the queen of spades.

South should, of course, have played a second club from hand at trick four without touching the spades.

63. Putting it all together

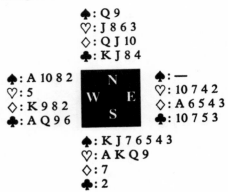

♠: Q 9
♡: J 8 6 3
◇: Q J 10
♣: K J 8 4

♠: A 10 8 2
♡: 5
◇: K 9 8 2
♣: A Q 9 6

♠: —
♡: 10 7 4 2
◇: A 6 5 4 3
♣: 10 7 5 3

♠: K J 7 6 5 4 3
♡: A K Q 9
◇: 7
♣: 2

Once East has shown up with the ace of diamonds, the rest of the missing high cards can be placed with West for his opening bid. These are the ♠A, ◇K, ♣A and ♣Q.

Why didn't West open with a bid of 1 NT on his thirteen points? Clearly because his hand is unbalanced.

But why did he open one diamond on what appears from the opening lead to be a four-card suit? Because he has no suit longer than four cards. Having an unbalanced hand with only four-card suits, West must have a 4–4–4–1 shape.

When you play a spade, if West plays low, you must finesse the nine to avoid two trump losers. If West started with ♠: A, ♡: 10 7 5 4, ◇: K 9 8 2, ♣: A Q 9 6 and the defence comes to a heart ruff, console yourself with the thought that you could not have prevented it.

On the actual hand, West could have defeated the contract by leading his singleton, but you have to concern yourself only with the defence put up at the table. The point is to avoid the automatic, mechanical, unquestioning play of a spade to the queen at trick three. Not everyone will believe it is a matter of bad luck.

64. Severing the connection

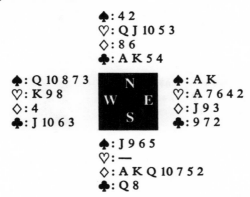

♠: 4 2
♡: Q J 10 5 3
◇: 8 6
♣: A K 5 4

♠: Q 10 8 7 3
♡: K 9 8
◇: 4
♣: J 10 6 3

N W E S

♠: A K
♡: A 7 6 4 2
◇: J 9 3
♣: 9 7 2

♠: J 9 6 5
♡: —
◇: A K Q 10 7 5 2
♣: Q 8

East must return a club at trick five to defeat the contract. South is known to have begun with two clubs (West led ♣3), four spades (he would have rebid the suit with five) and six or seven diamonds. It is almost certain that South has seven diamonds, for with a singleton heart he would hurriedly have discarded it on the clubs.

In fact East could have solved any problems by playing ♡A or a club at trick three. The diamond return was not fruitful, since East can always over-ruff dummy.

A diamond or heart return at trick five allows declarer to make the contract by a squeeze on West in the black suits. The play of the diamonds reduces West to ♠: Q, ♣: J 10 6, while dummy has ♡: Q, ♣: A K 5 and South has ♠: J 9, ◇: 2, ♣: 8. When South leads ◇2, West must unguard one of the black suits and declarer makes the rest.

The club return breaks up the squeeze by cutting off the declarer from the club menace in dummy.

65

Rubber, dealer West,
neither side vulnerable.

The bidding:

SOUTH	WEST	NORTH	EAST
	3 ◇	3 ♠	Pass
3 NT	Pass	Pass	Pass

♠: A K Q 10 4 3
♡: A 6 3
◇: 7 4
♣: Q 7

♠: 6
♡: 9 7 4 2
◇: A K 5
♣: A 9 6 4 3

The play:
West leads ♡K. Plan South's play.
(If South ducks in dummy, West continues with the queen of hearts
and then the jack of hearts. East following suit each time.)

66

Teams, dealer South,
North-South vulnerable.

The bidding:

SOUTH	WEST	NORTH	EAST
1 ♠	Pass	2 ♡	Pass
2 NT*	Pass	3 ♣	Pass
3 NT	Pass	Pass	Pass

♠: 7
♡: K 8 7 6 4
◇: K 6
♣: Q J 8 7 2

♠: J 6 4
♡: A J 5
◇: 9 8 7 4 2
♣: 9 3

* 15–17 points

The play:
1 West leads ◇3: six, seven, **queen**
2 South leads ♣5: six, **queen**, nine
3 ♣2 is led from dummy: three, king, **ace**
4 West leads ♡Q: king, **ace**, three
5 **East leads ♡J:** nine, two, four.

How should East continue?

67

Rubber, dealer South,
North-South vulnerable.

♠ : A 9 8 6 2
♡ : 9 5 2
◇ : 6 4 3
♣ : 7 5

The bidding:

SOUTH	WEST	NORTH	EAST
2 ♣	2 ♠	Double	Pass
3 ♣	Pass	3 NT	Pass
6 ♣	Pass	Pass	Pass

♠ : —
♡ : A K J 4
◇ : A K Q J
♣ : A K Q J 3

West leads ◇10, won by the ace. The trumps turn out to be 3–3, and West discards a spade on the third diamond.

How should South play?

68

♠ : J 10 9
♡ : K Q J 4
◇ : J 3
♣ : K 7 5 3

♠ : K Q 5 3
♡ : 8
◇ : K 9 5
♣ : Q 10 9 8 6

Dealer South,
both sides vulnerable.

The bidding:

SOUTH	WEST	NORTH	EAST
1 NT*	Pass	2 ♣	Pass
2 ◇	Pass	3 NT	End

* 15–17 points

The play:
1 West leads ♣10: three, *East discards ♡2*, **jack**
2 South leads ♡7: eight, **king**, five
3 ◇J is led from dummy: ace, two, five
4 East leads ♠6: seven, **queen**, nine.

How should West continue?

65. Counter move

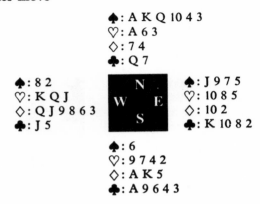

♠: A K Q 10 4 3
♡: A 6 3
♢: 7 4
♣: Q 7

♠: 8 2
♡: K Q J
♢: Q J 9 8 6 3
♣: J 5

♠: J 9 7 5
♡: 10 8 5
♢: 10 2
♣: K 10 8 2

♠: 6
♡: 9 7 4 2
♢: A K 5
♣: A 9 6 4 3

South should not expect the spades to break evenly, so he should hold up the ace of hearts in an attempt to preserve an entry for the spades.

The defence does best by continuing hearts to knock out the entry. If the declarer wins the first or second round of hearts, he will fail.

Once West has shown up with the king, queen and jack of hearts, declarer can be confident that East will hold the king of clubs. After winning the third round of hearts he should cash the ace and king of diamonds, eliminating East's holding in the suit, and then play the spades from the top down. When East wins the fourth round of spades, he will be forced to lead away from the king of clubs.

On the actual hand, this line of play produces ten tricks. If East happens to have five spades, the end play in clubs gives the declarer his ninth trick.

66. Haste makes waste

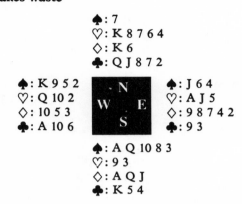

♠: 7
♡: K 8 7 6 4
◇: K 6
♣: Q J 8 7 2

♠: K 9 5 2　　　　♠: J 6 4
♡: Q 10 2　　　　♡: A J 5
◇: 10 5 3　　　　◇: 9 8 7 4 2
♣: A 10 6　　　　♣: 9 3

♠: A Q 10 8 3
♡: 9 3
◇: A Q J
♣: K 5 4

At the table East woodenly returned a diamond, giving the declarer an easy passage. Dummy's king won, a third heart was played, and the defenders made only three hearts and a club.

Had East returned a spade at trick six, that would have established a fifth trick for the defence.

After the hand East complained about West leading such a poor suit, but that was unreasonable for the bidding made a diamond lead almost mandatory from the West hand. East also argued that he could not tell whether West had ◇A or ♠K, but his reasoning does not stand up. If West held ◇A he could always cash it when in with the third round of hearts, whereas if West held ♠K he needed a spade lead from East.

Even if South has a strong spade hand, as good as ♠: A K Q 9 8, ♡: 9 3, ◇: Q J 10, ♣: K 5 4, he cannot succeed on a spade return. The ♡10 is, of course, marked with West because of South's failure to support hearts at any time.

67. Let them do your work for you

                    ♠: A 9 8 6 2
                    ♡: 9 5 2
                    ◇: 6 4 3
                    ♣: 7 5

♠: K Q J 7 5 4 3   ♠: 10
♡: 6   ♡: Q 10 8 7 3
◇: 10 9   ◇: 8 7 5 2
♣: 8 6 2   ♣: 10 9 4

                    ♠: —
                    ♡: A K J 4
                    ◇: A K Q J
                    ♣: A K Q J 3

South should play off the fourth diamond and his two remaining trumps, taking care to retain the three hearts in dummy. Then cash the ace of hearts and exit with the four of hearts.

In most positions the defenders will be endplayed, for a spade return will concede the contract at once while a heart return will run into South's tenace.

On this line of play South is bound to make the slam whenever (a) West has the ten of hearts, with or without the queen, (b) either defender has a doubleton honour, and (c) either defender has a singleton or void in hearts.

A problem will arise only when East has 10 x x or Q 10 x x. Then on the heart return at trick twelve declarer will have to make the right guess to land his contract.

68. Beggars can't be choosers

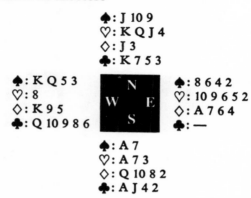

```
              ♠: J 10 9
              ♡: K Q J 4
              ◇: J 3
              ♣: K 7 5 3
♠: K Q 5 3              ♠: 8 6 4 2
♡: 8          N        ♡: 10 9 6 5 2
◇: K 9 5    W   E      ◇: A 7 6 4
♣: Q 10 9 8 6  S       ♣: —
              ♠: A 7
              ♡: A 7 3
              ◇: Q 10 8 2
              ♣: A J 4 2
```

West must continue with a low spade, dropping South's doubleton ace. The defenders then make three spades and two diamonds before declarer can come to his ninth trick in diamonds.

It should not be too hard for West to find this play. He has ten points, dummy has eleven, and South is marked with at least fifteen for his opening bid of one no trump. East cannot therefore have more in high cards than the ◇A already seen. South has four heart tricks, three clubs and the ace of spades, and, given time, he will establish his ninth trick in diamonds (he would scarcely have led the jack unless he had the ten as well as the queen).

West cannot be sure that the ace of spades is doubleton, but he knows that this is the only chance for the defence. Necessity is the mother of accurate defence.

Bouquets are due to both declarer and partner; to South for crossing to dummy to lead a diamond rather than leading the suit from his own hand and to East for rising with the ace of diamonds (if he plays low, the contract cannot be beaten). Are bouquets also due to you as West?

69

Dealer South,
both sides vulnerable.

♠: J 6
♡: A K 9 4
◇: A 6 3 2
♣: 5 4 2

The bidding:

SOUTH	WEST	NORTH	EAST
1 NT	Pass	2 ♣	Pass
2 ♡	Pass	4 ♡	End

♠: A 8 3
♡: 10 6 3 2
◇: K 7
♣: A Q 10 8

The play:
1 West leads ◇10: **dummy's ace wins**
2 ♣2 led from dummy: nine, ten, **king**
3 West leads ◇Q: **king wins**
4 South leads ♡2: seven, **ace,** five
5 ♣4 is led from dummy: jack, **ace,** three.

How should South continue?

70

Dealer West,
neither side vulnerable.

♠: K Q
♡: A K 6 4
◇: K 8 6
♣: K Q 9 7

The bidding:

SOUTH	WEST	NORTH	EAST
	Pass	1 ♣	1 ◇
1 ♠	Pass	2 NT	Pass
4 ♠	Pass	Pass	Pass

♠: A J 4 2
♡: 7
◇: A J 10 7 3 2
♣: 6 2

The play:
1 West leads ◇9: six, ten, **queen**
2 South plays ♠3: seven, king, **ace.**

How should East continue?

71

Teams, dealer East,
North-South vulnerable.

The bidding:

WEST	NORTH	EAST	SOUTH
		1 ♡	2 ◇
5 ♣	5 ◇	End	

♠: 9 8 6 2
♡: A 10 5 4
◇: 10 6 3
♣: A 5

♠: J 7 4
♡: K 3 2
◇: A K Q 9 8 4 2
♣: —

The play:
1 West leads the ♡J . . . .

Having luckily escaped a spade lead, how should South play?

72

Teams, dealer South,
neither side vulnerable.

The bidding:

SOUTH	WEST	NORTH	EAST
2 NT*	Pass	3 NT	End

*22–24 points, balanced

♠: Q 6 5
♡: 8 3 2
◇: 10 7 5 4
♣: Q 10 5

♠: A K 7 2
♡: 9 6 4
◇: K
♣: 8 7 6 4 2

The play:
1 West leads ♡5: two, four, **king**
2 **South plays** ◇A: two, four, king
3 South plays ◇8: **queen,** five, *East discards* ♣2
4 West leads ♠J: queen, **king,** four.

How should East continue, with the ♠A or the ♠2?

The solution is a matter of logic, not guesswork. No merit for answers
unsupported by reasons.

69. Keeping control at all times

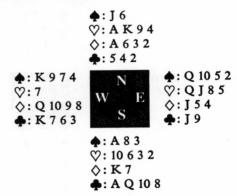

```
                    ♠: J 6
                    ♡: A K 9 4
                    ◇: A 6 3 2
                    ♣: 5 4 2
  ♠: K 9 7 4            N            ♠: Q 10 5 2
  ♡: 7            W         E        ♡: Q J 8 5
  ◇: Q 10 9 8         S            ◇: J 5 4
  ♣: K 7 6 3                         ♣: J 9
                    ♠: A 8 3
                    ♡: 10 6 3 2
                    ◇: K 7
                    ♣: A Q 10 8
```

At the table South continued with a second trump, a seemingly innocuous play, but when East turned up with Q J x x in trumps the contract could no longer be made. East ruffed the third club and drew a third round of trumps, leaving South with only nine tricks.

South should foresee the danger of a 4–1 trump break and should continue clubs at trick six. East may ruff and return a trump, but the declarer is in full control and makes ten tricks by playing on cross-ruff lines.

There is no danger when the trumps are 3–2, even if the third club is ruffed by the short trump hand. Declarer wins the return, draws a second round of trumps and proceeds with the cross-ruff, losing at most two trump tricks and the king of clubs.

70. Deep is the tangled web

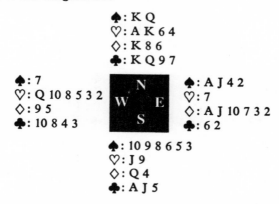

```
              ♠: K Q
              ♡: A K 6 4
              ◇: K 8 6
              ♣: K Q 9 7
♠: 7                        ♠: A J 4 2
♡: Q 10 8 5 3 2             ♡: 7
◇: 9 5                      ◇: A J 10 7 3 2
♣: 10 8 4 3                 ♣: 6 2
              ♠: 10 9 8 6 5 3
              ♡: J 9
              ◇: Q 4
              ♣: A J 5
```

The best return at trick three is the two of clubs, the play East would make if he had a singleton club. South is marked with six spades for his jump to game, so to look for a diamond ruff is futile. But see what may happen if South thinks you have a singleton club.

South wins the club, plays a spade to the queen and receives the bad news. At this point, in order to guard against fraud, he should cash one top heart and then play the king of diamonds to prepare a safe way back to his hand. But he may well overlook the precaution of cashing a high heart and exit immediately with the king of diamonds. If he does, you have a good chance of defeating the contract. Take the ace of diamonds and continue with the ◇J. South will ruff and lead the ten of spades to your jack. Now play the seven of hearts and declarer will be stranded in dummy, wondering whether to come back to hand with a club or with a third-round heart ruff. If he guesses wrong and continues hearts (he probably will), you have the setting trick.

It is worth noting that this deception would have had no chance if you had played ace and another diamond at tricks one and two. Declarer would later have discarded a heart on the king of diamonds, thus preparing a safe way of returning to hand.

71. Hope for the best

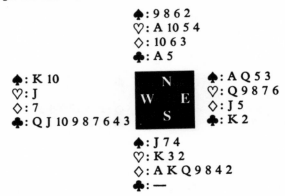

♠: 9 8 6 2
♡: A 10 5 4
◇: 10 6 3
♣: A 5

♠: K 10
♡: J
◇: 7
♣: Q J 10 9 8 7 6 4 3

♠: A Q 5 3
♡: Q 9 8 7 6
◇: J 5
♣: K 2

♠: J 7 4
♡: K 3 2
◇: A K Q 9 8 4 2
♣: —

No doubt North should have doubled five clubs (although the defenders have to cash their tricks very precisely to beat the contract), but you need not concern yourself with might-have-beens.

You need something favourable to happen in the spade suit. The best chance is to win the ace of hearts, play ♣A throwing a spade, ruff the second club, draw trumps (you need to find them 2–1) and then exit with a spade.

The ♠7 is the better exit card as it increases the chance of West playing low from A x, K x or Q x. You hope that after winning the second spade the defenders will be endplayed. A club will give you a ruff and discard, while a heart from East will run to the ten.

There are many positions where you will succeed, with spades either 3–3 or 4–2, although you may have to pick the position. For example, in the above diagram when a spade is led, West wins and continues with spades. East overtakes and returns a low spade, and you have to decide whether he began with A x x or A Q x x—not too difficult though the position isn't certain (he could have opened on ♠: A x x, ♡: Q x x x x, ◇: J x, ♣: K Q x).

72. Point count reveals shape

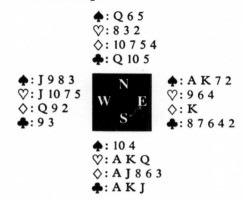

♠: Q 6 5
♡: 8 3 2
◇: 10 7 5 4
♣: Q 10 5

♠: J 9 8 3
♡: J 10 7 5
◇: Q 9 2
♣: 9 3

♠: A K 7 2
♡: 9 6 4
◇: K
♣: 8 7 6 4 2

♠: 10 4
♡: A K Q
◇: A J 8 6 3
♣: A K J

If West began with ♠: J 10 x, you must continue with the ♣2 to avoid blocking the suit. But if the spade position is as in the above diagram you just continue with ♠A to fell the ten. You cannot blame partner for making things difficult, for the ♠J from West is the only card to give the defence a chance.

How can East work out which situation actually exists? He should reason as follows: (a) West's lead places South with at least three hearts. (b) South's approach to the diamonds indicates a five-card holding, and this is confirmed by West's ◇2 on the first round. (c) The three top hearts plus ace and jack of diamonds add up to only fourteen points, therefore South must have a further eight points in clubs (A K J) to make up his quota of twenty-two. It follows that South can have only two spades. The answer is the same if we give South the jack of hearts instead of the jack of clubs. Again he can have only two spades.

East must therefore continue with ♠A at trick five. The hand is fascinating in that it is one of the rare cases where a defender can deduce the shape of declarer's hand by counting his points.